Discover the rich heritage of Korea's treasured traditional spirits and the bold new cocktails redefining their future.

In *Korean Cocktails*, beverage director Haera Shin invites you into the vibrant world of Korea's treasured traditional alcohols, known collectively as sool. From soju, the country's best-known spirit, to makgeolli rice wine, these time-honored drinks carry centuries of craft and culture—and are now being reimagined by a new generation of makers and mixologists around the globe.

Featuring 76 inventive recipes, Shin teams up with some of the most exciting bartenders in New York, Los Angeles, Seoul, and Singapore to showcase the delicious diversity of sool alongside the complex flavors of the Korean pantry. The refreshing Hechi Highball highlights omija, Korea's five-flavor berry. The rich, creamy Dalgona transforms the viral coffee sensation into an indulgent cocktail, and the Nabak Soju captures the spice and funk of homemade kimchi. Alongside these originals, you'll find bold riffs on classics like the fiery K-Margarita, nutty Sesame Manhattan, and bright, herbaceous Perilla Mojito, plus large-format and zero-proof drinks to ensure there's something for every occasion. Complete with striking color photographs and recipes for cordials, syrups, and infusions, *Korean Cocktails* is a vibrant tribute to Korea's drinking culture and a must-have for the modern bar.

KOREAN COCKTAILS

KOREAN COCKTAILS

FROM TRADITIONAL SPIRITS TO MODERN DRINKS

HAERA SHIN

Countryman Press

An Imprint of W. W. Norton & Company
Independent Publishers Since 1923

CONTENTS

INTRODUCTION

What comes to mind when I think of Korean cocktails?

To the rest of the world, they might not have the same historical cachet that the phrase "American craft cocktails" calls to mind, or evoke the minimalist, technique-driven associations that Japanese cocktails have earned. This is why it has taken some 10-plus years into my career to distill what I believe the present and future of Korean cocktails look like. In Seoul, New York, LA, and other international cities, Korean cocktail bars are gaining prestige and creating some of the most unique interpretations of classic cocktails by showcasing native ingredients. The time is now for Korean-inspired cocktails to make their mark on the world stage.

I did not realize this right away, but all the years in the kitchen with my mother—a young Korean emigrant to New York—paved the way for my cocktail point of view. The conscious seed for this idea began 10 years ago, when I was working as a bar manager at Zuma, a now internationally acclaimed, high-end, modern Japanese izakaya. The first location had opened in London in 2002, and I was hired as an opening bartender for their sophomore location in New York. Today, the group boasts 29 locations across the globe. Their bar program marked a significant leap from my previous gigs behind the stick. Practicing Japanese mixology instilled me with technique and discipline. During the preopening training process, we perfected ice carving, cutting down monolithic ice blocks with band saws to perfect cubes and then using paring knives and ice picks to chip them into spheres. We practiced rounds of blind drink building behind the service bar, where you had to build drink tickets and not look down at your rail—not only did you have to know exactly where the rhubarb cordial was, you had to ensure the first and last drink built were perfectly timed. The cocktails were like swans: graceful to behold, concealing the relentless effort beneath the surface, much like the extensive prep required to create the final product. The required discipline weeded out those who were only there to clock in, make a quick buck, and clock out. After eight months, I was promoted to bar manager and continued to hone my own aesthetic. At a certain point during my tenure at Zuma, I asked myself: Pomp and circumstance aside, what makes a person truly enjoy drinking a cocktail? To me, the best cocktail has a harmonious balance of flavor: sweetness, acid, and a touch of bitterness or umami. Similarly, Korean cuisine captivates our senses because it strikes that perfect balance.

This, I came to understand, is what I had learned in my mother's kitchen. Korean seasoning ingredients were just as familiar to me as salt and pepper. I recognized that my mother, who emigrated to the United States at 20 years old and raised us in New York in her early 20s, did the monumental task of acclimating to an unfamiliar country while soothing her homesickness through food. The first thing she did was learn how to cook everything she and my father missed from home. I watched her make everything from scratch: She pickled every kind of vegetable; made vats of kimchi; roasted seaweed; sautéed and stored assorted banchan; cooked soups, braises, and stews. Anything she could not find in New York, she smuggled in from Korea on her trips back and forth throughout the year.

Korean food can emit strong odors, so there was the regular, main kitchen refrigerator with all our "American food" and the sidepiece refrigerator that housed all things Korean. This special refrigerator was both intimidating and fascinating to me while growing up—I never knew what sort of sea creature I would find in a stage of advanced fermentation. The Korean pantry is filled with ingredients that need to serve a multitude of purposes. Many of them are fermented over time to enhance shelf life and develop the rich umami flavors that define the Korean palate. As I grew older, I realized the benefit of knowing how every building-block ingredient tasted and recognized the alchemy that happened when these ingredients were combined.

Summering in Korea every year as a child left an indelible mark on my sense of flavor and cultural identity. The months I spent with my cousins are among my most cherished memories. We wrapped our fingertips in crushed bongsoonga flowers, staining them a vivid red that lasted the length of our stay. We ate watermelon sprinkled with salt and instant coffee, and turned tomatoes into dessert with a dusting of sugar. We made pilgrimages to Hyundai Department Store for towering bowls of bingsoo—shaved ice piled high with red beans and any topping we could dream of. After swimming in the lake, we sat on the forest floor around open flames, grilling kalbi. On the walk home from piano lessons, we sucked on Chu Chu Bar ice pops. Every morning started with a bottle of Yakult. I loved nothing more than wandering the aisles of Korean convenience stores, mesmerized by the colorful packaging of snacks and drinks. Being immersed in my native

land during those formative summers created a deep, lasting connection that stayed with me long after I returned to the States.

At Zuma, I used these memories of the flavors of my upbringing to draw cocktail inspiration from, blending nostalgia with innovation. When a cocktail called for a touch of sweetness, I reached for cheong and yeot, traditional Korean sweeteners, to add depth and complexity to the drink. Cheong is a syrup that incorporates a vegetable or fruit with equal parts sugar, and yeot is glutinous rice sugar.

When I joined Momofuku in 2018, I felt as though I had finally captured the white whale of my career. I became part of the opening management team, as beverage manager, for their second Noodle Bar location, in Columbus Circle. I had long admired Momofuku's reputation for stripped-down dining, letting the product speak for itself. There was a transgressive, anarchic quality to their approach to food and beverage, particularly at restaurants like Ko and Ssam Bar. As a guest, I recall dining at a moody, dimly lit Ssam Bar on Second Avenue, and then pivoting to their adjoining bar, Booker and Dax, where I was blown away by the level of cutting-edge cocktails being churned out in such a small space. I became a huge fan of the bar alumni at Momofuku: Don Lee, Dave Arnold, John deBary. To get to be in a creative role after them was the most exciting prospect of my career at that point.

When I joined, my mentor Jake Lewis gifted me a high-tech highball tap system in which I could create carbonation in completed format, dispensed out of tap handles at the optimal carbonation level (50 psi in the keg to achieve 15 psi in the glass after inevitable CO_2 expulsion), dilution (15 to 20 percent, depending on viscosity), and temperature (as cold as fucking possible). Once the nerdy science stuff was under my belt, the combinations were endless. I feature some of these creations in a make-at-home format in this book. (I also credit Jake with my late bloom into wine, which has evolved into an obsessive personal and professional passion.)

In 2021, I had the opportunity to further advance my career with Momofuku during the wake of the pandemic shutdown. I was now in the position to oversee the reopening of multiple locations as beverage director. The time I spent with our team while COVID-19 was still a terrifying daily reality, opening restaurants in previously never-seen-before incarnations, was a collective exercise in creativity, flexibility, fear conquering, and blind faith. In 2021, Ssam Bar shuttered its doors, only to emerge in a larger, splashier space under the guidance of the endlessly talented chef Eunjo Lee. With a Korean executive chef at the helm, I was able to create my first completely Korean cocktail program. It's a testament to Momofuku that this was wholeheartedly embraced and unquestioned. My first cocktail, the K-Margarita, could not be taken off the menu without complaints and is also featured in this book (page 183).

> "The goal of this book is to bridge the Korean culture of drinking with the mastery of Korean ingredients."

It was also during this time that I dove deep in to premium craft Korean spirits, particularly through the portfolio of Kyung Moon Kim. Master Sommelier Kim was the first importer I encountered who brought in meticulously curated premium spirits he personally sourced from Korea. When we spoke recently, when I told him about my book, he informed me, "The Korea premium sool movement just started fifteen years ago and exploded in the last five years." His mission is to connect people with truly well-crafted products after nearly a century of mass-produced soju dominating the market. He understands this shift won't happen overnight. When asked how he decides what to distribute, he explained that he looks for "a flavor profile that is unique, not overlapping with what is already out there. Spirits made with rice or wheat or barley, they taste very different from each other and different producers treat rice and grain differently, and diversity is important." Kyung supports new brands wherever he can and notes the recent stream of up-and-coming labels, which he feels is a great sign for progress in terms of sool entering the global marketplace. He also gives priority to working with brands that have a proven track record of longevity and history.

As a beverage director overseeing multiple outlets, you serve as both buyer and arbiter, selecting the products that shape your beverage programs and define your backbar. These decisions come from a deep understanding of your clientele and demographic, paired with diligent research and curation. It's your responsibility to seek out the best spirits and wines—those that not only taste exceptional but also carry a story worth sharing, reflecting the passion of their producers. My connection to my native country has always been a point of pride, and it's one of the reasons I've been committed to championing the unique spirits of Korea. While not as globally recognized as, say, sake, Korean fermented beverages are crafted with extraordinary care, history, and singular character—qualities that deserve far greater appreciation and visibility on the world stage.

Over the past decade, through the many places I've worked that gave me a platform to share my creations, I've built a repertoire of recipes that I'm excited to share in this book. The timing could not be better. In today's culinary landscape, Korean cuisine has become increasingly mainstream, and in the past five years it has garnered significant recognition within fine dining circles. New York restaurants Jung Shik and Atomix both retain two-star Michelin status: Jung Shik received theirs in 2021 and Atomix in 2019. Korean pantry ingredients like gochujang and doenjang are more widely recognized and easier to source for home cooking. It is common to see big-box supermarkets carry multiple varieties of kimchi in their produce section. Frozen food sections stock bulgogi bowls, Korean mandoo (dumplings), and if you were on TikTok in the past year, you likely witnessed the viral sensation of Trader Joe's kimbap rolls, which quickly sold out across the United States.

Thanks to the advocacy of professionals like Kyung Moon Kim, premium Korean spirits can now be seen peeking out from behind many backbars in the States. Particularly soju. The ubiquitous green bottle used to be the sole representation of Korean soju, but now there is much more diversity. Premium soju, as well as makgeolli, chungju, and bokbunja offer unique bases for inventive cocktails. Even in markets where these spirits aren't readily available, I've organized pop-up collaborations featuring such brands as Jinro Soju and Tokki Soju, and artisanal makgeolli, to introduce and celebrate these dynamic flavors in spaces where people might not otherwise encounter them.

The goal of this book is to bridge the Korean culture of drinking with the mastery of Korean ingredients, in their many delicious quaffable forms, as exemplified through modern cocktails. The first section includes a brief overview of the history of sool and its different types, alongside an exploration of Korean drinking culture. Next, you will find key elements of the Korean cocktail pantry as well as information on building your bartending toolbox.

The chapters that follow organize cocktails by their flavor profile and format. Should you be on the hunt for something boozy, you can find it in "Spirit Forward," or if you want something fizzy and fun, you can find it in "Highballs." The cocktails are diverse and I hope you will find one that really hits the mark for you. As for the recipes, I certainly could not do it alone. The diversity of Korean flavors and cocktails merits a diversity of lenses, and so this book includes my own recipes and those of my talented friends who are also making strides to bring Korean ingredients to the fore. Their recipes are included at the end of each chapter.

1

KOREAN COCKTAIL FUNDAMENTALS

한국 칵테일 필수품

雪中
百歲酒
一般蒸溜酒
眞心
Jinsim
홍삼주
Hong Sam Ju
19% by Vol. 375ml
Product of Korea
사춘

KOREAN SOOL

The general word for "alcohol" in Korean is "sool." This word encompasses thousands of native sool varieties that exist in Korea. You will typically find that most sool is distilled or brewed with rice and then fermented with nuruk, a native yeast akin to koji in Japan. Koreans historically enjoy sool that has clean, neutral flavors, but they enjoy sweeter, more fruit-forward sool as well. Most specific names for sool end with "-ju."

Although the earliest records of formalized sool brewing date back to the 12th century, during the Goryeo Dynasty, brewing likely began much earlier. It was around the 14th century that standardized brewing methods were introduced and sool became widely consumed. As it seems is often the case, it is through the resources of religious avenues, in this case, through Buddhist temples, that sool was produced in large quantities, which was then served and sold in local pochas (inns). During the succeeding Joseon Dynasty, Korea experienced a 500-year period of immense prosperity, which saw the development of many foundational elements of Korean culture, etiquette, societal norms, language, and government structure. During this time sool continued its expansion. It was not only widely consumed but also commonly brewed at home. Many of the traditional sool known today originated during the Joseon Dynasty, and several of them will be highlighted throughout this book.

Koreans are and have always been notoriously proud of and protective of alcohol created in Korea, and exports beyond the country did not even begin until the late 20th century. Recently, soju has increased its export into the States year over year, with 2025 slated to surpass $200 million. While soju and beer have a wide margin lead in alcohol export, smaller categories of sool are also gaining popularity and presence behind the bar. The clearest way to break down the categories of sool is in its two broadest forms: distilled spirits and fermented alcohols. Soju and all its varieties fall under the distilled spirit category, discussed on page 18. The fermented category can be further broken down into three subcategories: takju, yakju, and gwasilju, each of which has its own variations.

TAKJU

Takju is made by filtering fermented grains, such as rice, through a sieve, leaving behind particles of sediment, resulting in its characteristic cloudy, milky, and opaque appearance. Makgeolli is the most popular in this category.

MAKGEOLLI

Makgeolli is the earliest Korean alcoholic beverage on record. This special alcohol was first brewed by rice farmers in celebration of the harvest. They would hold back some rice from each harvest with the express purpose of turning it into makgeolli. During those days, makgeolli was made by milling the rice by hand and then cooking it with water into a porridge. At this point, nuruk was introduced to the mash. Nuruk was made by shaping steamed wheat or barley into cakes and letting them dry naturally. The drying process would catch all the wild yeast, mold, and microorganisms from the surrounding air and trap them for future activation. The cakes would be left to develop for weeks or months before being utilized as a fermentation starter for the mash. Once the nuruk and mash were combined and left in a moderately warm environment, the yeast would activate and eat the sugars to create alcohol and CO_2. Makgeolli made this way would have a delicious, slightly sweet, and slightly effervescent body to it, with a signature milky, pale color.

Today, the focus has shifted to small-batch, handcrafted brews made with traditional fermentation and local ingredients, moving away from mass production. Modern makgeolli goes beyond classic flavors, incorporating fruit, herbs, spices, and even espresso to create distinctive profiles. Production has even made its way stateside—Hana Makgeolli is a Brooklyn-based small-batch brewery producing innovative blends with flavor infusions such as omija ("five-flavor berry") and elderflower. Màkku Makgeolli is produced in Korea but is owned by a New Yorker (and friend) named Carol Pak, who is canning hers with such flavor infusions as coffee and mango. Makgeolli can be a wonderful addition to cocktails, to add body and texture along with the flavors from their infusions.

YAKJU

Yakju is made by clarifying fermented rice wine by removing the sediment that would be present in takju. The flavor is more complex and nuanced, as usually different herbs or flavors are added to the mixture. Chungju and baekseju are the most popular in this category.

CHUNGJU

Chungju is a rice wine with origins that date back to the Goryeo Dynasty. Back in those days, it was consumed during jesa, a ceremony still practiced today, which is the tradition of bowing, praying, and offering food and drink to one's ancestors during the anniversary of their death or during Lunar New Year. The word itself can be directly translated to mean "clear alcohol." The simplest way to look at chungju is as being clarified makgeolli that is on its way to becoming soju if further distilled. The process entails fermentation in much the same way as makgeolli, but chungju goes through a further process of distillation through a hybrid still, starting with a copper still and finished in a column still. Like whiskey and other spirits, the heads and tails are disposed of postdistillation, leaving the purest liquid in the middle to be bottled, usually 10 to 14 percent ABV.

Chungju flavors are extremely versatile, depending on the producer. They can be aged or steeped in special herbs. The purest flavor of chungju is a touch savory, but often has a sweet, delicate finish. I enjoy using chungju as a substitute for dry vermouth. A well-known chungju I often use is called Yangchon chungju. Yangchon utilizes locally grown rice that is cultivated without herbicides by releasing snails into the fields. The resulting umami flavor of this particular chungju recalls shiitake mushrooms or cheese rinds. It is great served neat, paired with meat-centric dishes, but I love using it in cocktails to add a touch of umami without any saltiness.

BAEKSEJU

The direct translation for "baekseju" is "100-year wine," referring to the medicinal properties in the herbs that are infused into the wine and the notion that, by drinking it, you can live to be 100 years old. Baekseju is made from glutinous rice, nuruk, and a variety of herbs, including ginseng, ginger, cinnamon, omija, and others. Baekseju is usually vinified to about 13 percent ABV, making it a very sippable option to serve with food. People sometimes drink baekseju by mixing it with soju; this is called osipseju, which translates to "50-year wine," recalling the idea that bumping up this wine with soju can make a stiffer drink, but one that cuts the life-lengthening properties in half. I love to use baekseju in cocktails, such as a seasonal autumn or winter spin on an old-fashioned or a Manhattan.

GWASILJU

Gwasilju is a fruit wine made by fermenting fruits into a wine or by mixing fruit with sugar and alcohol. The resulting wines can range from dry to sweet—and, at the risk of sounding redundant, fruity, depending on the source of fruit used. Bokbunja-ju and maesil-ju are the most popular in this category.

BOKBUNJA-JU

Bokbunja-ju is a Korean fruit wine made from wild or cultivated black raspberries. It was first mass-produced and bottled for export by Bohae in 2004. Korean black raspberries are vinified by crushing and mixing the fruit with water, then fermented with yeast to produce alcohol. The resulting wine has a rich, fruity taste with a distinct raspberry flavor and is mildly sweet.

One of my favorite aspects of this wine is the origin of the name. Let me preface this by saying, Koreans have many myths about what sorts of ingredients bring virility. The characters in the name translate to: bok ("flip") bun ("pot") ja ("the man"). As legend has it, a man was wandering in a forest, picking these black raspberries, and fermented himself a wine. He drank himself to sleep and, when he woke up, had to relieve himself; he did so with such force, he flipped the pot!

MAESIL-JU

Maesil is a small, green, tart fruit akin to a plum or apricot. They are too sour to eat raw, but make a deliciously floral and plummy alcoholic beverage. Made simply, maesil that has been left out to dry for a day is added to soju that is slightly sweetened with sugar or honey and left for several weeks or months to macerate and incorporate the flavors together. Maesil-ju is often enjoyed as a digestif or as one would enjoy a dessert wine.

SOJU

"Soju" translates to "burnt liquor," referring to the technique of distillation that was first introduced when Korea was invaded by the Mongols (1231–59), who brought with them the Middle Eastern distillation techniques they had learned from the Persians. The Mongols learned to make arak, which is a distillate of grapes and anise. This technique was applied to native Korean grains, such as rice, barley, and wheat, to create soju. As stated in the introduction, this practice was further standardized over the next 200 years. Soju had remained a drinking staple from that point forward, using rice until around the 1950s, during the Korean War, when rice was banned from soju usage due to rationing and was replaced with cheaper, easier-to-grow products, such as sweet potatoes or tapioca, for many years. It was only during the 1990s that the ban was lifted, and rice was able to be used again. Soju had to win its reputation back after many years of cheaply produced, high-volume production.

GREEN BOTTLE SOJU

The history of green bottle soju is a fascinating one. In the 1990s, Doosan Beverage began mass-producing soju in green bottles, choosing the color to symbolize freshness and vitality, as well as to help

preserve the liquid inside. As the trend caught on, other companies adopted the same style of bottle to capitalize on its growing popularity. Rather than compete, these companies eventually collaborated, agreeing to standardize and share the green bottles to reduce costs and promote eco-friendliness. Today, Jinro Soju—the leading soju brand—emphasizes the significance of the packaging, stating, "The green bottle is a powerful symbol of soju's heritage and connection to nature and purity."

FLAVORED SOJU

Flavored soju is your cocktail's secret weapon. Traditionally, green bottle soju has been the staple in Korean drinking houses and restaurants. But in recent years, flavored varieties have sparked some controversy. Critics often dismiss them as overly sweet or synthetic tasting, while fans appreciate their ability to soften harsh alcohol notes and their lower ABV. Personally, I love using them to amplify existing fruit flavors in cocktails. I think of them less as cordials and more as fruit extracts, because they deliver an intense, focused burst of flavor, like a laser beam of strawberry when you use strawberry soju.

PREMIUM SOJU

In the last 10 years, there has been a premium soju boom. The difference is in the ingredients used and the production process. Premium soju producers begin by sourcing local organic rice and wheat. They then often use column stills over continuous stills, which take longer, but result in a cleaner, or more sophisticated product. Smaller production means smaller yields, but much more attention to detail. Premium sojus can be aged in smaller containers called onggi, which are clay pots used in the production of jang (fermented soybean products). The porous clay allows for a bit of oxidation, which allows the raw spirit to soften and inherit more depth of flavor. One of the first premium sojus I had was Tokki Soju, which was founded in 2016 in Brooklyn by Brandon Black and Douglas Park. It was a revelation to see soju produced beyond Korea, and with the added attention to detail of sourcing glutinous rice and using no additives at all—and to top it all off, good old-fashioned Brooklyn water.

KOREAN DRINKING CULTURE

Korean drinking style has always put the social aspect first. Historically, Korean drinking establishments in Korea and the United States were casual and low frill. "Pocha" is the term for a casual drinking establishment. Koreans always center their drinking on food first. The idea of a bar where the primary draw is a cocktail is a more recent development. Usually at these pochas, alcoholic beverages were simply imbibed in the form of bottles of soju and beer. The vibe was made more convivial with drinking games played with empty bottles of soju—such as Spin the Bottle and Tell a Truth, or to flick the tab on the soju lid back and forth and the loser drinks. Interactive elements to taking your shot always got more fun the more you drank: Chopsticks lined up, shot glass on top, make your somaek (soju bomb) all the more dramatic. These days, everyone knows about "APT," the drinking game made famous by K-pop idol Rosé and Bruno Mars. You start by chanting "Ah-pah-tuh" six times, then the person whose turn it is calls out a number and then everyone stacks their hands in the middle. When the count ends, the person whose hand is at the top must drink.

There is also a very specific way in which Korean people drink with one another. I recall early memories of my dad and his buddies getting together after golf at our house on Saturday evenings. It was my first exposure to the social discourse of drinking. There were usually multiple green bottles of soju surrounding an array of dried fish, squid, nuts, and cut fruit. The dining room was loud, boisterous, and jovial. Every now and then, the room would fall silent as one of my dad's friends would stand up with a bottle, the sign that everyone had to finish what was left in their shot glass because it wasn't an option to deny a pour. Everyone would raise their comically small shot glasses with two hands as a sign of respect. Even this was particular—the bottom of the shot glass was placed on the open left hand, holding the glass with the right hand. After everyone was poured, the sudden exclamation of "Gunbai!" was loudly made in unison, breaking the silence, then everyone would resume their loud carousing.

Korean drinking etiquette is practiced among friends, family, colleagues, and even between couples on dates. The etiquette practiced depends on representations of gender and of age. When receiving a drink from an older individual, one must turn one's head and drink away from the table as a sign of respect. This also applies to women in the presence of men, regardless of age. As out of date as most think these practices are, being socialized with this feeling of always respecting one another when drinking affected me, especially as I moved into bartending as a career. Signs of respect are hugely important in my profession, to making sure that the aspect of hospitality is an important and enjoyable part of being in a communal drinking atmosphere.

Korean nightclubs (called "night" for short) are extremely popular venues for young people to gather and socialize. In earlier decades, class and gender constructs made it difficult for men and women to approach each other in a romantic context within professional and social spaces. In the 1970s, "booking," a forced method for encouraging individuals of the opposite sex to interact, was prevalent in nightclubs. Booking was a way to break the ice by enlisting servers to invite women from their tables to join men who had requested their presence. When technology caught up, "phone-ting" was a variation on "booking," whereby telephones were placed at tables and the men could call other groups of interest directly. This practice has almost completely died down, but it was all the rage until the advent of social media and dating apps.

You might think that growing up in New York would have distanced me from traditional Korean drinking practices, but I was surrounded by many first-generation Koreans who embraced this culture. I frequently visited Korean bars and clubs in Flushing and Koreatown, where the drinking style was proudly upheld. Even though we were being raised in the States, my peers and I were still deeply connected to these traditions. I also had unnis and oppas (older female and male friends, respectively) to whom I was expected to show respect. And as an unni to two younger sisters myself, I was equally accustomed to being treated with deference for my age. It was a matter of pride. My parents wanted us to be Americanized but were fiercely protective of their Korean roots. I had to attend Korean school after regular school, and one of my favorite pastimes was watching K-dramas with my mom—back then, rented on bootleg VHS tapes recorded at the local Korean grocery store. Those dramas often featured traditional Korean drinking, and as a kid, I absorbed those scenes. As I grew older, I found joy in living out those rituals myself.

MODERN COCKTAILS

Over the past decade, Korea's cocktail culture has gained international recognition, with bars consistently earning praise from global industry awards. Most recently, Bar Cham was ranked no. 2 in Asia by *World's 50 Best Bars*. Pine & Co., Bar Pomme, Alice Cheongdam, and Charles H. have also been celebrated with various accolades over the past five years, each prioritizing innovation while staying rooted in Korean identity. These programs have pushed the envelope of what would have been taboo only a decade ago. During a recent visit to Antidote Bar in Seoul, a much-loved cocktail destination that builds its menu around "prescription" and carries the theme through such details as a Florence flask or Erlenmeyer beaker as glassware, I ordered a cocktail called Weed, which was accompanied by a lit lavender joint rolled in a roach clip. The aromatics were meant to be enjoyed alongside the cocktail. Antidote,

Bar Cham, Pine & Co., and many other bars of similar acclaim have graciously contributed their recipes to this book.

Alongside this rise of modern cocktail programs, the highball has secured its place as a staple. Borrowed from Japanese cocktail culture, where it holds iconic status, the classic highball of Japanese whisky, soda, and lemon has become a formula for many different iterations. I feature some of my own highball creations in the following chapter.

unsweetened. They are very versatile and so thirst quenching! If you ever find yourself in the tea aisle of your local Korean grocery store, there are so many other teas you can experiment with, including lotus leaf, pine needle, persimmon leaf, and goji. They often lend themselves to steeping into spirits to bring another dimension.

CHEONG AND YEOT

Korean cuisine is rooted in resilience and necessity and is a result of centuries-old practices of preservation of ingredients for year-round use when seasonally unavailable.

CHEONG: Like fermentation, cheong extends the life of seasonal fruits and vegetables with sugar, ensuring their flavors can be enjoyed throughout the year. A syrup or preserve is made by fermenting or macerating ingredients like fruits and vegetables in sugar or honey. Over time, the mixture develops into a rich, flavorful syrup that can be used as a sweetener, marinade, or flavor enhancer in various dishes and drinks. It is often used as a tea base and is still widely considered to be a remedy to treat the common cold or other minor illnesses. Originally, the word "cheong" referred to honey used in royal court cuisine. Since then, it has become the term for any type of sweetener made with this process. Maesil-cheong is made with Korean plums and is similar to Japanese ume. Yuja Citron Honey, as it is referred to on English packaging labels, is a staple in many Korean pantries. Yuja (known as yuzu in Japan) peels are cured for a minimum of six months with honey and sugar to create a fragrant base. It is most often used in tea and is celebrated for immune-boosting properties due to its high vitamin C content—approximately two-and-a-half times that of lemon juice. See page 33 for a recipe to make your own cheong with any kind of fruit.

YEOT: Similar to cheong, "Yeot" refers to sweeteners made with boiled-down grains, such as rice, corn, or barley. Ssal-yeot (rice syrup) is commonly used in banchan to add sweet stickiness to finish dishes. Oligo yeot, traditionally made from corn or sweet potatoes, is less sweet than simple syrup. Its consistency resembles the viscosity of honey, offering a smooth, glossy thickness, yet its neutral flavor allows it to enrich drinks with body and sheen without overwhelming them with excess sweetness.

GAMTAE/GIM

Gim is a type of seaweed that is widely used in Korean cuisine, often served wrapped over rice. Gamtae is a rare and special variety of gim that can only be found in the southern coastal waters of Korea. It grows naturally in uncontaminated seawater and cannot be farmed, making it difficult to source. Gamtae has a distinctive flavor profile, marked by deep salinity, rich umami, and subtle notes reminiscent of truffle.

GOCHUGARU

Gochugaru is chile flakes made from ground, sun-dried Korean red chiles. It is the most important seasoning used in kimchi. The flavor has heat, but it is also fruity and smoky as well.

JANG

Jang encompasses several fermented soybean products. They are traditionally made by fermenting soybeans with bacteria and then pounding and kneading them into bricks, which are then dried into what is called meju. The meju is then rehydrated and processed in various ways, described as follows.

DOENJANG: Doenjang is made with meju as the main building block. The meju is introduced to a brine and softens into a paste that is aged in earthenware pots (known as onggi) until it develops into a rusty brown color. It is similar to miso but way funkier.

GANJANG: Ganjang is Korean soy sauce and is traditionally made by adding meju to water, turning the meju into a dark liquid. Ganjang differs slightly from Japanese soy sauce, in that it utilizes more soybeans during the process, resulting in a slightly nuttier profile. Either one is perfectly fine to use in any of these recipes.

GOCHUJANG: Gochujang is a thick red paste made from meju, with the addition of gochugaru. This spicy red paste is used to flavor soups and stews.

KKAESOGEUM

Roasted sesame seeds and salt are combined into a seasoning that is used everywhere in Korean cooking. It adds salinity and nuttiness, and Koreans are nutty for it.

KKAENNIP

Perilla leaf, which has a fragrant, slightly lemony, bitter taste, is often described as a cross between basil and mint. Perilla leaves are used in various ways, including as ssam (wraps for meat and rice), chopped into salads, and pickled as banchan (side dishes). It is a great substitute in cocktails that call for mint or need an herbaceous lift.

SESAME OIL

Sesame seeds are toasted and then pressed to extract the oil. The result is a nutty, roasty, toasty flavor that is often used as a finishing oil on top of dishes.

TOOLS OF THE TRADE FOR THE HOME

Having the right tools is essential for re-creating drinks accurately. Professional-grade tools ensure consistency, allowing cocktails to taste exactly as intended by the recipe. Fortunately for home bartenders, bar tools are now highly affordable and stylish enough to be proudly displayed on your home bar cart or in your kitchen.

BAR TOOLS

METAL SHAKING TINS: The standard large size is 28 ounces, and the small one is 18 ounces. While you don't need Koriko Japanese tins—the industry favorite and ones I use behind my bars—it's crucial to find tins with these exact sizes and weighted bottoms, for stability during drink preparation. If possible, test the seal by capping them together; you should hear a suction sound and a satisfying snap when released. These sizes are ideal because, when filled with ice, the length from one end to the other allows for optimal aeration during a hard shake.

MIXING GLASS & BARSPOON: These can get pricey, but you don't have to spend a lot—though it is a fun opportunity to pick out the glass etching or design that speaks to you. Just be sure you keep it clean and dry and safely stored. My bars are littered with a graveyard of hairline-fracture mixing glasses from bartender use. As for barspoons, they come in countless handle designs, allowing you to showcase your personality. Look for one with a long, thin handle that allows smooth, effortless movement of ice around the glass.

HAWTHORNE, JULEP STRAINER & FINE-MESH BAR STRAINER: The Hawthorne strainer (with the coil of wire) is meant to strain the liquid from your shaking tins, and the julep strainer is meant for your mixing glass. When a recipe calls for the use of a fine-mesh bar strainer, it is in reference to a handheld mini strainer. You use a bar strainer to catch any errant solids, such as ice, fruit pieces, or herbs from a cocktail after it has been shaken or stirred, ensuring a smooth and clean final drink.

JIGGERS: Having two jiggers is best: one with 2-ounce and 1-ounce measurements, and another with ¾-ounce and ½-ounce measurements. This guarantees the exact measurement in every cocktail.

FOR SERVING

GLASSWARE: Most of the glassware in these recipes is standard for all bars and is likely already part of your housewares. The recipes in this book call for collins, coupe, highball, martini, Nick & Nora, old-fashioned, rocks, shot glasses, or wineglasses. Korean-style serving vessels can be easily procured online. Makgeolli is traditionally served in metal teapots along with metal serving bowls, a practice rooted

in history, when farmers enjoyed the drink after a hard day's labor. The durability and lightweight nature of metal made it ideal for outdoor use. It is also fun to play with different traditional bowls to serve cocktails in. Rice bowls, or a stone pot, can be a striking serving vessel, so have fun with it!

ICE BLOCKS & SPEARS: It isn't mandatory to have specialty ice shapes; however, there is a reason behind their use. Compared to standard ice cubes, solid ice blocks and spears melt slower and reduce the dilution rate of a cocktail such as an old-fashioned. They are also aesthetically pleasing.

If you really want to stun, you can make your own blocks and spears at home with a technique made widely popular by Dave Arnold in his book *Liquid Intelligence*. It requires a few handy tools that you can purchase online: A 5-quart Coleman cooler with the lid off can fit in a typical home freezer, and a serrated knife and claw ice pick will suffice. Fill the cooler with water and allow it to freeze, uncovered, for 24 hours. Because the cooler is insulated, it will not let the ice freeze all the way to the end. The open-ended cooling technique, called directional freezing, allows the air bubbles to escape and keeps the frozen part of the ice crystal clear. Once most of the block is frozen, you can remove it from the cooler and carve it into your desired shape.

PREP & STORAGE TOOLS

CHINOIS & CHEESECLOTH: A chinois serves the same purpose as a fine-mesh bar strainer, but on a larger prep scale, with its fine perforations ensuring that batches are smooth, uniform, and free of unwanted solids. Cheesecloth is used for the most delicate straining tasks and can easily be layered inside a chinois to capture finer particles. It's especially useful for a technique called fat-washing. For example, in a recipe in the book, alcohol is fat-washed with sesame oil by combining the ingredients and freezing them for several hours. The sesame oil solidifies, but the alcohol does not. The fat can be strained out, leaving the flavor and the texture behind, minus any greasiness or oiliness. When straining, the solids to cling to the cheesecloth more effectively than to metal alone.

MEASURING CUP & GRADUATED CYLINDER: A standard Pyrex measuring cup works great for measuring liquids of all temperatures. A graduated cylinder is best for measuring smaller increments, as ingredients for some of the component recipes in this book are broken down into milliliters.

GRAM SCALE: Some of the prep recipes require precise measurements, and for home bartenders, a gram scale will be useful for accurately weighing smaller quantities.

QUART CONTAINERS & BATCHING BOTTLES: These containers are commonly used in bars for storing prepped batches or as vessels for making syrups and infusions. Quart containers are typically the ideal size for prepared ingredients scaled for home use. Batching bottles in the 750 milliliter size are also perfect for storing syrups or cocktail batches during preparation.

GLASS DROPPER BOTTLES & BITTERS BOTTLES: The small glass dropper bottles with eyedropper dispensers range from 2 to 4 ounces and contain enough liquid to dispense a tiny drop into your cocktail. When a cocktail calls for saline or bitters, it's important to add it in controlled, small doses, and squeezing the dropper handle allows for precise, measured additions. Just so you can get an idea of how small we are talking, a standard eyedropper holds about 1 milliliter of liquid, which is equivalent to 20 drops, and often you will be adding 3 to 4 drops of liquid to your cocktail.

Tincture or bitters bottles are usually made of glass and shaped into all sorts of designs with a dasher top. The dispensing part of a bitters bottle allows for a bit more liquid than an eyedropper, an amount referred to as dashes. One dash of bitters is about 0.5 milliliter of liquid. Often a recipe will call for 3 or 4 dashes of bitters.

MACHINERY

SODA SIPHON & CO_2 CARTRIDGES: This is a great investment for any home bartender. If you love fizzy drinks and regularly enjoy soda water, this is the perfect way to enjoy them at home and crafted with flavors from your imagination. You can also control the amount of bubbliness in a soda you make, by adding CO_2 at your discretion. A 1-liter dispenser is all you need, in addition to accompanying CO_2 cartridges.

CREAM WHIPPER & N_2O CARTRIDGES: Another great investment, for making instant whipped cream from anything dairy or nondairy based. It is the best tool to use for topping drinks as the nozzle dispenses a controlled amount that will give that professional look. Cream whippers require N_2O cartridges. In the absence of a cream whipper, you have the option to use a stand mixer or hand mixer and a bowl.

HIGH-SPEED BLENDER: This is an important bar tool that is used for many purposes. The obvious one is for blending all sorts of different ingredients into a smooth liquid. It can also be used to break down such ingredients as nuts, seeds, or dried herbs into a fine powder. If you are able to procure one, the standard-bearer in high-speed blenders is Vitamix, which is a professional-grade blender known for its powerful motor, durability, and ability to handle a wide range of tasks, including crushing ice, with ease.

2

HIGHBALLS

하이볼

JUSTICE OF THE PEAS

SERVES 1

When I first joined Momofuku, I was given an incredible opportunity to develop highballs for their batched highball program. The lineup featured four highballs on tap, but executing them at the necessary volume was a challenge and an extremely rewarding exercise in team coordination. Each highball required two corny kegs filled with the cocktail—one connected to the CO_2 injection phase and the other, already carbonated, tapped for dispensing. A backup cocktail always had to be ready on tap, as force-carbonating a 5.2-gallon keg takes 24 hours. This highball was one of my first creations for the spring lineup. It showcases the bright, fresh flavors of snap peas and perilla, resulting in a crisp, vegetal, and irresistibly crushable drink. Sugar snap peas are at their sweetest during spring.

1½ ounces Snap Pea and Perilla Soju (recipe follows)
½ ounce Noilly Prat or other dry vermouth
¼ ounce Dolin Génépi le Chamois
¼ ounce Citric-Malic Solution (page 32)
Top: 2 ounces Singha soda
Garnish: 3 snap peas

Combine all the ingredients, except the soda and garnish, in a mixing glass filled with ice. Stir and strain into a collins glass with an ice spear. Top with the Singha soda and garnish with 3 fanned-out snap peas on a skewer.

SNAP PEA AND PERILLA SOJU

MAKES 1 CUP

1 cup Solsongju Damsoul pine soju
90 grams snap peas, chopped roughly
5 grams perilla leaves with stems

Combine all the ingredients in a quart-size container and steep for 24 hours at room temperature. Strain out and discard the peas and perilla, then store in the refrigerator for up to a week.

NAMSAN GARDEN

SERVES 1

Inspired by Seoul's beloved Namsan Outdoor Botanical Garden, I wanted to capture a garden in a glass. Incorporating cucumber and mint with ginseng soju gives this cocktail a well-rounded expression of verdant, floral, and herbaceous flavors. It's my refreshing ode to nature in the heart of the big city.

3 or 4 cucumber coins

3 or 4 fresh mint leaves

¾ ounce Koryo Sambiju ginseng soju

½ ounce Vicario Dragoncello liqueur

½ ounce St-Germain elderflower liqueur

¼ ounce Ming River Baijou

1 barspoon freshly squeezed lime juice

Garnish: 1 cucumber ribbon, cut with a vegetable peeler

Top: 2 ounces Fever Tree tonic water

Muddle the cucumber coins and mint leaves in a mixing tin. Combine the four spirits and the lime juice and shake vigorously. Strain into a highball glass with an ice spear. Wrap the cucumber ribbon around the inside of the glass. Top with the tonic water.

MA PÊCHE

SERVES 1

Many of my cocktail recipes involve steeping tea in a spirit, to bring an extra dimension to a cocktail. This cocktail utilizes jasmine tea, which imparts a fragrant floral element to the gin it is steeped in. My recent love of gin was propelled by my discovery that gin and tonics are actually the perfect highball. My hat in the ring is this version of the gin and tonic, embellished by flavors of peach soju and maesil-cheong, which is a green plum syrup. Maesil is often used in lieu of sugar in savory Korean dishes like bulgogi, kimchi, and salad dressings. The name of the cocktail is an ode to one of Momofuku's restaurants.

- 1½ ounces Jasmine-Infused Gin (recipe follows)
- 1 ounce Jinro or other peach soju
- ½ ounce maesil-cheong
- ¼ ounce Citric-Malic Acid Solution (page 32)
- Top: 2 ounces of your favorite tonic water
- Garnish: 1 Firestix edible flower, or 1 lemon twist

Combine all the ingredients, except the tonic water and garnish, in a mixing tin with ice and shake. Strain into a highball glass with fresh ice. Top with the tonic water. Garnish with a Firestix or lemon twist.

JASMINE-INFUSED GIN

MAKES 2 CUPS

- 7½ grams loose jasmine tea
- 2 cups Sonbi gin

Steep the tea in the gin in a large container for 4 hours at room temperature. Strain out the tea, rebottle the gin, and store in a cool, dry place for up to a month.

NOTE: This gin can also be used in lieu of a plain gin and tonic.

MELONS FROM H-MART

SERVES 1

This is a cocktail I created for a spring/summer lineup at Majordomo, one of Momofuku's LA concepts. I always loved the fresh, slightly sweet and juicy flavor of Korean melons (chamae), which have a distinctive fragrance and muskiness that is a cross between just-ripe honeydew and cucumber. Here, Good Day watermelon soju as well as Dragoncello, a tarragon liqueur, complement and enhance the melon juice. Calpico is a probiotic Japanese soft drink made with fermented milk. The flavor is like a citrus yogurt and adds both body and brightness to cocktails. This highball also works with watermelon juice, if chamae is unavailable.

- 1 ounce Hwayo 41 soju
- 1 ounce Good Day or other watermelon soju
- ¼ ounce Vicario Dragoncello liqueur
- 1½ ounces Chamae Juice (recipe follows)
- ½ ounce Calpico
- ¼ ounce Citric-Malic Solution (page 32)
- 2 dashes Saline Solution (page 33)
- 1 teaspoon absinthe, in an atomizer
- Garnish: 1 chamae slice

Combine all the ingredients, except the absinthe and garnish, in a shaking tin with ice. Shake and strain into a collins glass over ice cubes. Spray the absinthe with an atomizer and top with a chamae slice, to trap the absinthe mist.

CHAMAE JUICE

MAKES 2 CUPS

- Equipment: juicer or blender
- 2 to 3 medium chamae (Korean melons)

Wash the melons, halve one, and slice a few pieces for garnish. Then, cut the rest into cubes. No need to peel the skin or remove the seeds; the whole fruit is edible. Add the segments to a juicer, juice, then strain to remove the fibers. Store in a container in the refrigerator for up to 3 days.

PERILLA MOJITO

SERVES 1

If one herb could represent Korea, it would be perilla, or as it is called in Korea, kkaennip. It is often used in wraps called ssam and is also pickled into kimchi and added to soups. The flavor is minty, herbaceous, and slightly aniselike. Because it is basically the mint of Korea, it merited the mojito treatment. This version uses a technique of blending the herb and spirit in a high-speed blender. The speed and precision of the blender ensures that the perilla is cut without bruising, and the citric acid is added to retain the color so it doesn't brown.

1½ ounces Perilla-Infused Rum (recipe follows)

¾ ounce freshly squeezed lime juice

½ ounce ginger yuja cheong

Garnish: 2 or 3 perilla leaves

Combine all the ingredients, except the garnish, in a shaking tin with ice. Shake vigorously and then strain into a collins glass with ice cubes. Garnish with the perilla leaves, pressed between the ice and the glass.

PERILLA-INFUSED RUM

MAKES 1 CUP

Equipment: high-speed blender

½ cup perilla leaves, stems removed

1 cup Flor de Caña 4 Year Extra Secco white rum

¼ teaspoon Citric-Malic Solution (page 32)

Combine all the ingredients in a blender and pulse three or four times to break down and incorporate the leaves into the liquids. Let rest for 2 hours, then fine-mesh strain into a bottle and store in the refrigerator for up to a week. Note: Roughly chopping the leaves with a knife is also an option.

HECHI HIGHBALL

SERVES 1

Omija, a.k.a. the "five-flavor berry," offers a unique balance of sour, sweet, salty, bitter, and spicy or pungent notes. Omija is a favorite in Korean cuisine, where dishes are celebrated for hitting all these flavor profiles at once. Jangsu Omijaju is a delicate wine vinified from omija berries, with a neutral-grain spirit added to enhance its signature five-flavor complexity. To further highlight omija in this cocktail, the rhubarb syrup incorporates omija tea, for which the dried berries are steeped to extract their rich flavors. The cocktail is named after Hechi, a pink mythical bear that is the official mascot of Seoul.

1½ ounces Soonhari or other yogurt soju

1 ounce Jangsu Omijaju

¼ ounce Giffard Vanille de Madagascar liqueur

1½ ounces Rhubarb Omija Syrup (recipe follows)

Top: 2 ounces club soda and Vanilla Yakult Foam (recipe follows)

Garnish: food-safe begonia flowers (optional)

Combine all the ingredients, except the club soda, Vanilla Yakult Foam, and the garnish, in a highball glass. Fill with ice, top with the club soda. Give the cocktail a quick stir to incorporate all the ingredients. Finish with a layer of Vanilla Yakult Foam. Garnish with begonia flowers, if desired.

continues →

OMIJA POWDER

MAKES 30 GRAMS (FOR 2 COCKTAILS)

10 grams dried whole omija
20 grams sugar

Using a spice grinder or food processor, grind the omija into powder and mix with the sugar. Store in a sealed container in a dry place.

OMIJA AND STRAWBERRY-INFUSED SOJU

MAKES 1 CUP

1 cup Tokki Soju Black
130 grams fresh or frozen strawberries
18 grams dried whole omija

In a resealable plastic bag, mix together the soju, strawberries, and omija. Refrigerate for 24 hours. Strain through cheesecloth and bottle. Store in the refrigerator.

PERILLA AND MAGNOLIA

DYLAN "KENZO" HAN OF FIRSTBORN, LOS ANGELES

SERVES 1

Dylan Han says of this delicious highball, "I've always loved delicate, aromatic, highball-style cocktails. Perilla leaves are simultaneously refreshing and savory, so they are a perfect flavor to use in that style of drink. I also found the Jangsu Omijaju at Flask & Field, a Korean-owned wine and spirits store in LA, and the berries have a ton of nuance similar to sloe berries, which are a common cocktail ingredient. The Classic Laddie's honey and floral notes integrate easily without overpowering the other elements and add honey and malted layers." Omija has multiple names. Botanically called the schisandra berry, it is also commonly known in English as magnolia berry. Omija's literal translation is "five-flavor berry" due to its flavor profile of sweetness, sourness, bitterness, saltiness, and pungency.

- 1¼ ounces Perilla-Infused Scotch (recipe follows)
- ¾ ounce Jangsu Omijaju
- ½ ounce freshly squeezed lime juice
- ¼ ounce Simple Syrup (page 32)
- Top: 2 ounces club soda
- Garnish: 1 fresh perilla leaf

Combine all the ingredients, except the club soda and garnish, in a shaking tin filled with ice. Hard shake and strain into a tumbler over ice. Top with the club soda and garnish with the perilla leaf.

PERILLA-INFUSED SCOTCH

MAKES 1 CUP

- 30 grams perilla leaves
- 1 cup Bruichladdich "The Classic Laddie" or preferred unpeated Scotch whisky

Blanch the perilla leaves in water in a saucepan. Strain and then add to the whisky; steep at room temperature for 3 hours. Strain out the leaves and store the scotch in a bottle in the refrigerator for up to 2 weeks.

3

BRIGHT & REFRESHING

밝고 상쾌한

KOREAN AIR

SERVES 1

This cocktail I created for my first program at Noodle Bar is an elegant spin on the classic Aviation cocktail. The crème de violette is dialed down a bit here to make room for a more plummy flavor profile brought forward by Won Mae liqueur and maesil cheong. Won Mae has more of a floral plum note, while the maesil brings a jammier plum note. The flavors are reflected in the cocktail's vibrant color, brought on by the unmistakable tint from steeped butterfly pea flower.

- 1 ounce Butterfly Pea Flower–Infused Gin (recipe follows)
- ¾ ounce The Han Won Mae plum liqueur
- ¼ ounce maesil cheong
- ¼ ounce crème de violette
- ½ ounce freshly squeezed lemon juice
- 1 small barspoon egg white
- Garnish: 1 food-safe lavender sprig

Combine all the ingredients, except the garnish, in a shaking tin with ice and shake until well chilled. Double strain into a Nick & Nora glass. Garnish with the lavender sprig.

BUTTERFLY PEA FLOWER–INFUSED GIN

MAKES 1 CUP

- 1 cup Sonbi gin
- 2 grams dried butterfly pea flower buds (can be purchased online)

Combine the ingredients in a container. Steep for 30 minutes. Strain and store in a bottle in the refrigerator for up to 2 weeks.

JEJU SUNRISE

SERVES 1

Ninome tangerine soju, a unique soju from Jeju Island, blends rice, volcanic rock water, and locally grown, sun-dried tangerine peels. To build on the orange flavor in the soju, I add Sac Sac orange, a popular drink made from mandarins that includes the fruit pulp, which pops in your mouth when you drink it. And because tangerines and mandarins have a delicate and sweet flavor, Aperol and Mommenpop Blood Orange liqueur are added to bring a bit of a bitter edge. Jeju Island, often referred to as the "Hawaii of Korea," is renowned for its incredible variety of citrus fruits. The island's volcanic soil provides ideal conditions for their cultivation. And the sunrises are glorious.

- 1½ ounces Ninome tangerine soju
- ¼ ounce Lillet Blanc
- ¼ ounce Kook Soon Dang baekseju
- ¼ ounce Bigallet China-China liqueur
- 2 ounces Sac Sac orange
- Top: 2 ounces tonic water, ½ ounce Mommenpop Blood Orange liqueur, and ½ ounce Aperol
- Garnish: 1 orange wedge

Combine all the ingredients, except the tonic water, Mommenpop, Aperol, and garnish, in a shaking tin and shake vigorously. Strain into a highball glass filled with ice, then top with tonic water.

In a separate tin, combine the Mommenpop Blood Orange and Aperol. Gently pour the mixture down the side of the glass; it will sink to the bottom. Garnish with an orange wedge on top of the drink.

PERSIMMON'S CUP

SERVES 1

Pimm's Cup is a classic cocktail I enjoy when I want to feel like a posh Brit. It is heavily imbibed during Wimbledon and there is a reason. It is super-refreshing and fruity but also slightly bitter, so you feel quenched when you take a sip. It is also a low-ABV cocktail, so you can technically crush them all day. In my version, persimmons and Korean pear juice are added to the fruit mixture by swapping out the ginger ale for a homemade soda. Also, the Pimm's is slightly cut with Seoul Night, a South Korean plum soju that's double distilled and cold-filtered and has a 23 percent ABV.

- 1 ounce The Han Seoul Night plum soju
- 1 ounce Pimm's
- ½ ounce Apologue Persimmon Bittersweet liqueur
- Top: 3 ounces Persimmon Pear Soda (recipe follows)
- Garnishes: 1 dehydrated persimmon slice, plus 1 pineapple frond or mint sprig

Combine all the ingredients, except the Persimmon Pear Soda and garnishes, in a shaking tin with ice and shake until well chilled. Strain into a metal cup and top with the Persimmon Pear Soda. Top with crushed ice and garnish with a dehydrated persimmon slice and pineapple frond (or a mint sprig if a frond is not available).

PERSIMMON PEAR SODA

MAKES 2 CUPS

- Equipment: soda siphon, 2 CO_2 cartridges
- ½ persimmon, sliced
- ½ cup Korean pear juice (store-bought or homemade)
- 2 cups water
- 25 grams sugar
- 10 grams fresh mint leaves

Combine all the ingredients in a pot and a simmer until the sugar is dissolved and the persimmon becomes soft, 5 to 7 minutes. Strain into a container and store in the refrigerator until well chilled. Pour the liquid into a soda siphon and infuse with two CO_2 cartridges.

NOTE: This soda can also be enjoyed on its own over ice.

BAD BUNNY

SERVES 1

"Tokki" means "rabbit" in Korean, so of course this brand of soju had to be combined with carrots to create this spring cocktail, which implements carrots in two ways. Carrots are dehydrated and then rehydrated in soju. Because many fruits and vegetables contain a high water content, when added directly to another liquid, not much flavor is extracted. However, dehydration concentrates their flavors by removing water. When rehydrated in a liquid like soju, these concentrated flavors are released more effectively, maximizing the infusion. Ginger, passion fruit, and honey round out the cast.

1 ounce Carrot-Infused Soju (recipe follows)

1 ounce Ålander Nordic rum

½ ounce ginger honey tea

1 ounce carrot juice (store-bought or homemade)

½ ounce passion fruit juice

2 ounces ginger beer

Garnish: ½ baby carrot with green top

Combine all the ingredients, except the ginger beer and garnish, in a shaking tin with ice and shake until well chilled. Strain into a rocks glass with ice cubes. Add the ginger beer. Garnish with the baby carrot half.

CARROT-INFUSED SOJU

MAKES 1 CUP

Equipment: oven or dehydrator

5 medium carrots, sliced into ½-inch coins

1 cup Tokki Soju Black

Dehydrate the carrots at 115 to 125°F for 6 hours or overnight in your oven or a dehydrator. Store in an airtight container until ready to use.

Measure 21 grams of dehydrated carrots, place in a container along with the soju, and steep in the refrigerator for 24 hours. Strain and store in the refrigerator for up to 2 weeks.

GZB

SERVES 1

"GZB" is a slang term derived from the Korean word "gijibae," which loosely translates to "badass bitch." The term was popularized by K-pop star CL, who uses it as a loving way to refer to her fans. It perfectly captures the energy behind this cocktail, which I created for a soju program at Nowon in NYC. Designed with the ladies in mind, this drink is pretty, pink, and dangerously easy to sip.

1 ounce yogurt soju
1 ounce Hwayo 53 soju
1 ounce Boiron lychee puree
½ ounce Cherry Cordial (recipe follows)
Top: 2 ounces dry sparkling rosé
Garnish: 1 cherry

Combine all the ingredients, except the wine and garnish, in a shaking tin filled with ice. Shake until chilled and strain over ice into a stemless wineglass. Top with your favorite dry sparkling rosé and garnish with the cherry.

CHERRY CORDIAL

MAKES 1½ CUPS

Equipment: high-speed blender
85 grams pitted red sweet cherries (14 to 15 cherries)
1 cup water
1½ ounces Mancino Sakura vermouth

Combine the cherries and water in a high-speed blender and blend until finely pureed. Strain into a medium bowl through a cheesecloth-lined fine-mesh strainer. Add the Mancino Sakura vermouth and store in a bottle in the refrigerator for up to 2 weeks.

SUMMER OF GEORGE

SERVES 1

Created for the inaugural program for Ssam Bar's new location at the South Street Seaport, this is a crushable, tiki-style cocktail perfect for the summer. Doenjang adds body and umami, elevating the drink while bringing subtle fruity notes and a touch of salinity, which keeps you going back for more. Gamgyul is a Korean tangerine, grown in Jeju Island, which is known for its juicy and tangy citrus qualities. You may find it, imported, at your local Korean grocery store, but if not, clementines work great, too. The cocktail was affectionately named after the *Seinfeld* episode where George ends up in the hospital after a summer of excessive laziness.

1½ ounces 400 Conejos or preferred mezcal

½ ounce Aperol

½ ounce Domaine de Canton ginger liqueur

1 ounce pineapple juice

½ ounce freshly squeezed gamgyul or clementine juice

1 barspoon doenjang

Garnishes: 1 banana leaf and 1 pineapple wedge

Combine all the ingredients, except the garnishes, in a shaking tin filled with ice. Shake vigorously and strain over ice in a rocks glass. Garnish with the banana leaf and pineapple wedge.

GINSENG SPRITZ

SERVES 1

Ginseng was such an interesting ingredient for me while I was growing up. I was given it in tea form as a catchall cure for lethargy, lack of focus, and general malaise. Only later to find out it was also a stamina booster, which Koreans love to tell you about at inappropriate times. It resembles a human as it grows to maturity, which I suspect is the reason behind the old wives' tale of its stamina-boosting properties. As a kid, I drank it only for its health properties, like when your mom gave you a children's vitamin in the morning and you did not necessarily enjoy the flavor. Only later did I return to this ingredient as a flavor-boosting source to be used in cocktails. Ginseng has a licorice-sweet flavor with earthy undertones and is slightly bitter. Sort of like an Aperol Spritz, sort of like an Americano, this cocktail harnesses ginseng's ability to round out the overall profile for a deliciously bitter drink.

1 ounce Sonbi gin

¾ ounce Aperol

¼ ounce cream sherry, such as Lustau East India Sherry

1 ounce Ginseng Cordial (recipe follows)

Top: 2 ounces sparkling wine plus 1 ounce club soda

Garnish: 1 lemon peel

Combine all the ingredients, except the wine, club soda, and garnish, in a white wineglass. Stir over ice and top with the sparkling wine and club soda. Garnish with an expressed lemon peel.

GINSENG CORDIAL

MAKES 1½ CUPS

1 cup water

¼ cup Koryo Sambiju ginseng soju

120 grams sugar

6 grams dried red ginseng

5 grams citric acid

3 large lemon peels

1 cinnamon stick

Place all the ingredients in a pot, slowly bring to a simmer, and cook for 1 to 2 minutes. Remove from the heat and allow to cool to room temperature. Strain and store in the refrigerator for up to a month.

STRAWBERRY MAKGEOLLITA

SERVES 1

Strawberry meets margarita through the lens of makgeolli, resulting in a creamier take on the classic tart and refreshing cocktail. This version features a strawberry syrup infused with guji-cha—a traditional Korean tea made from dried goji berries, known for their tart, cranberry-like flavor and herbal finish. Widely enjoyed in Korea, this tea is believed to be a natural mood and energy booster.

1½ ounces Cimarron Blanco or preferred blanco tequila

½ ounce Jinro or other strawberry soju

½ ounce Sulseam Red Monkey makgeolli

½ ounce Strawberry Goji Syrup (recipe follows)

½ ounce freshly squeezed lime juice

Garnish: 1 lime wheel

Combine all the ingredients, except the garnish, in a shaking tin with ice. Shake vigorously into a rocks glass with ice. Garnish with the lime wheel.

STRAWBERRY GOJI SYRUP

MAKES 2 CUPS

Equipment: high-speed blender

1¼ cups water

85 grams sugar

75 grams strawberries, hulled and chopped

50 grams goji berries

2 lemon peels

½ ounce Hwayo 53 soju

Combine the water, sugar, strawberries, goji berries, and lemon peels in a medium pot and simmer for about 30 minutes. The goji berries should soften and expand. Remove from the heat and discard the lemon peels. Transfer the mixture to a high-speed blender and puree. Pour the liquid through a fine-mesh strainer into a container and use a spatula to press down to release the liquid. Once the mixture is finely strained, add ½ ounce of the soju to stabilize and keep it from oxidizing. Store in the refrigerator for up to a month.

APPLES NOT APOLOGIES

SERVES 1

An intensely apple-forward drink, this cocktail is perfect for sweater season or a carnival—it basically tastes like a caramel apple. Apple Sidra is a popular Taiwanese carbonated soda that can be found in most grocery stores. The word for "apple" in Korean is "sagwa," but in another context, "sagwa" means "apologies."

- 1½ ounces Hennessy cognac
- 1 ounce Soonhari or other apple soju
- ½ ounce Doenjang Apple Orgeat (recipe follows)
- ½ ounce lemon juice
- 2 dashes Angostura bitters
- Top: 1 ounce Apple Sidra
- Garnish: 1 cinnamon stick

Combine all the ingredients, except the Apple Sidra and cinnamon stick, in a shaking tin with ice. Shake and strain into a collins glass filled with crushed ice. Top with Apple Sidra and more crushed ice. Light a cinnamon stick, let burn until it smokes, then blow out the flame. Nestle the cinnamon stick in the crushed ice, smoking side up.

DOENJANG APPLE ORGEAT

MAKES 1½ CUPS

- Equipment: high-speed blender
- 1 cup Giffard orgeat syrup
- 5 ounces apple cider
- 25 grams doenjang

Combine all the ingredients in a high-speed blender. Blend until fully smooth; store in a bottle in the refrigerator for up to a month.

NOTE: The doenjang will settle, so give it a shake before using.

K-TOWN NIGHTS

SHARON YEUNG OF DAIJOUBU POP UP, VARIOUS LOCATIONS ACROSS THE UNITED STATES

SERVES 1

Proudly referred to as "a Super Asian Pop Up," Daijoubu Pop Ups are hosted by Sharon and her partner, Caer Maiko. They make superdope Asian-inspired cocktails and support Asian American culture in the bar industry through creative cocktails and networking.

- 2 lime quarters
- ½ ounce Ottogi Worcestershire Sauce
- ¼ ounce Yangnyeom Sauce (recipe follows), or scant ¼ ounce Ottogi Yang-Nyeom Sauce
- 2 ounce Jinro Chamisul Original Soju
- 1¼ ounces Strawberry Syrup (recipe follows)
- Garnish: 1 lime wedge (optional)

In a shaker tin, muddle the lime quarters in the Worcestershire and Yang-Nyeom sauces. Add the soju and strawberry syrup. Add ice and give it a short shake. "Dirty dump" into a Korean ceramic mug. Garnish with a lime wedge, if desired.

continues →

STRAWBERRY SYRUP

MAKES ½ CUP

4 ounces good-quality ripe strawberries, hulled and diced small

2 ounces sugar

Pinch of kosher salt

Place the strawberries and sugar in a small container with a lid and give it a good shake until the strawberries are completely covered. Let macerate on the countertop until the sugar is completely dissolved, approximately 30 minutes. Transfer the strawberries to a small pot and cook over low heat for 2 to 3 minutes, or until it turns into a jammy consistency. Strain the mixture through a fine-mesh strainer and press down on the fruit for maximum extraction. Finish with a very small pinch of the salt. Store in the refrigerator for up to 2 weeks.

YANG-NYEOM SAUCE

MAKES ¾ CUP

1 tablespoon ketchup

1½ teaspoons water

1½ teaspoons honey

1½ teaspoons mirin

1½ teaspoons sambal oelek chili paste

½ teaspoon Korean plum extract

¼ teaspoon light soy sauce

¼ teaspoon gochujang

¼ teaspoon light brown sugar

¼ teaspoon gochugaru

Place all the ingredients in a small bowl and mix thoroughly. Strain the mixture through a fine-mesh strainer and set aside.

ROSE OF SHARON

SOPHIA KANG, BARTENDER AT ONE NINETY BAR, SINGAPORE

SERVES 1

This drink is a twist on the Singapore Sling. Sophia Kang explains, "This cocktail is inspired by a Singapore botanical garden, specifically, the engravings of the Rose of Sharon and the Vanda Miss Joaquim, the respective national flowers of the Republics of Korea and Singapore. Placed together, the two floral images spring from the same center, symbolizing the interconnectedness and friendship between the two countries."

- 1¼ ounces Hibiscus-Infused Gin (recipe follows)
- ¼ ounce Cointreau
- 1 barspoon Muyu Vetiver Gris
- ¾ ounce fresh pineapple juice
- ¼ ounce Grenadine (recipe follows)
- 1 barspoon yuja juice
- Garnish: 1 half-moon dehydrated pineapple

Combine all the ingredients, except the garnish, in a shaking tin with ice and shake until well chilled. Strain into a coupe glass and garnish with the half-moon of dehydrated pineapple.

continues →

HIBISCUS-INFUSED GIN

MAKES 1 CUP

1 cup Jung One gin
2 grams dried hibiscus flower

Infuse the two ingredients overnight at room temperature. Strain, then store in a bottle in the refrigerator for up to 2 weeks.

GRENADINE

MAKES 1 CUP

½ cup pomegranate juice
150 grams fine sugar
7 grams pink peppercorns
75 grams pomegranate molasses

Combine the pomegranate juice and sugar in a saucepan and simmer until the sugar dissolves. Add the pink peppercorns and simmer for another 3 minutes. Remove from the heat. Add the pomegranate molasses, stir well, and set aside to cool down. Strain, then store in the refrigerator for up to a month.

SOJURITA

SUNGRAE CHOI, HEAD BARTENDER AT SEOUL SALON, NEW YORK

SERVES 1

When Sungrae Choi first learned Tommy's Margarita eight years ago, he found the idea of using agave syrup to highlight the agave notes of tequila to be truly groundbreaking. For this drink, he explains, "When creating a margarita with soju as the base, I thought mirin would be the perfect counterpart to agave syrup. To achieve a syruplike texture, a mirin reduction creates a syrup with a similar sweetness and consistency to agave syrup, but with a strong rice flavor and rich umami. The final result is a delicious margarita variation that accentuates the rice notes of soju while also featuring tropical flavors from banana and lime."

1¾ ounces artisanal soju (e.g., Mir 40 or Tokki Soju Black)
½ ounce Pierre Ferrand dry curaçao
½ ounce Giffard Banane du Brésil liqueur
¾ ounce freshly squeezed lime juice
2 barspoons Mirin Reduction (recipe follows)
Garnish: Salt for rimming

Combine all the ingredients in a shaking tin and shake vigorously. Strain into a salt-rimmed rocks glass with a large ice cube.

MIRIN REDUCTION

MAKES ½ CUP

1 cup mirin

Simmer the mirin until it reduces to about half of its original amount. Store in the refrigerator for up to a month.

KITE FLYING

CHELSEA KIM, SEOUL-BASED BARTENDER AND THREE-TIME WORLD CLASS KOREA TOP 10 FINALIST

SERVES 1

Chelsea Kim states that her refreshing Mule-style cocktail was inspired by Korean autumn and traditional flavors. "By blending coconut green tea–infused Hwayo soju, fresh persimmon, and ginger ale, this cocktail captures the airy, bittersweet sensation of flying a kite on a crisp fall day."

1½ ounces Coconut Green Tea–Infused Soju (recipe follows)

2 ounces Fresh Persimmon Juice (recipe follows)

½ ounce freshly squeezed lime juice

¼ ounce Simple Syrup (page 32)

Top: 2 ounces Fever Tree ginger ale

Garnish: 1 mint sprig

Combine all the ingredients, except the ginger ale and garnish, in a shaking tin and add six ice cubes. Shake vigorously but briefly, then pour all the contents, without straining, into a chilled julep glass. Top with the ginger ale. Garnish with crushed ice, the mint sprig, and a straw.

continues →

COCONUT GREEN TEA-INFUSED SOJU

MAKES 1½ CUPS

- 1 tea bag Harney & Sons Green Tea with Coconut
- One 375-milliliter bottle Hwayo 25 soju

Infuse the tea bag in the soju at room temperature for 24 hours. Remove the tea bag and refrigerate the infused spirit until ready to use, up to 2 weeks.

FRESH PERSIMMON JUICE

MAKES ½ CUP

- Equipment: high-speed blender
- 4 persimmons, quartered

Place the persimmons in a high-speed blender and puree. Strain the puree through a cheesecloth-lined chinois and store in the refrigerator until ready to use.

4

CREAMY & TEXTURED

부드럽고 질감있는

MANGO DAIQUIRI

SERVES 1

This is a cocktail from one of my pop-up collaborations with the amazing Ben Hopkins from Pitt's, who also contributed a cocktail of his own to this book (Boatfire Gimlet, page 185). The inspiration came from my love for Màkku mango makgeolli—I just knew it would shine in a daiquiri. Rhum Agricole is the perfect pairing, adding vibrant, tropical, grassy notes that beautifully complement the soft, creamy mango. To ensure the mango flavor stands out and the drink can be enjoyed year-round, I also included mango-flavored soju and Calpico.

1 ounce Rhum J.M or preferred rhum agricole

1 ounce Màkku mango makgeolli

½ ounce Soonhari or other mango soju

1 ounce Acid-Adjusted Mango Calpico (recipe follows)

¼ ounce agave

Garnish: 1 slice mango

Combine all the ingredients, except the garnish, in a shaking tin with ice; shake vigorously. Strain and serve in a coupe glass, garnished with a slice of mango.

ACID-ADJUSTED MANGO CALPICO

MAKES 1 CUP

1 cup mango Calpico

15 grams citric acid

Combine the ingredients in a medium bowl and mix with a whisk until the citric acid is completely dissolved. Keep refrigerated for up to 2 weeks.

GREEN DOKKAEBI

SERVES 1

A dokkaebi is a figure from Korean folklore; it's like a goblin or spirit that comes to visit you at night. My grandmother used to say that if you whistled after dark, you'd summon one to your door. This cocktail, which I created for Ssam Bar, blends plum and nokcha (Korean green tea, similar to matcha) for a flavor that's both playful and a little mysterious—just like the dokkaebi.

- 1¼ ounces The Han Seoul Night plum soju
- ½ ounce The Han Won Mae plum liqueur
- 1¼ ounces Green Peach Puree (recipe follows)
- 1¼ ounces Nokcha Cold Brew (recipe follows)
- 1 egg white
- Garnish: 1 teaspoon nokcha powder

Mix together all the ingredients, except the garnish, in a shaking tin without ice and dry shake. Add ice and shake until well chilled. Strain into a double rocks glass over ice. Dust the top with nokcha powder by placing it in a bar strainer and gently dusting it over the top.

continues →

GREEN PEACH PUREE

MAKES 4 CUPS

Equipment: high-speed blender

One 19-ounce jar Japanese green peaches

250 grams Simple Syrup (page 32)

17½ grams citric acid

Combine all the ingredients in a high-speed blender. Start on low speed and gradually increase to maximum speed until the mixture is smooth. Transfer to a quart-size container and store in the refrigerator for up to 2 weeks.

NOKCHA COLD BREW

MAKES 1 CUP

1 cup room-temperature water

3 grams nokcha powder

Combine the water and nokcha in a quart-size container and whisk until fully dissolved. Store in the refrigerator for no more than 3 to 4 days, after which the cold brew will oxidize, losing flavor and turning a muddy color.

GO GO MA!

SERVES 1

This cocktail is based on a widely enjoyed sweet potato snack called Goguma Mattang, for which chopped sweet potatoes are first roasted and then tossed in brown sugar syrup and topped with sesame seeds. It is usually enjoyed at the end of a meal, served with toothpick skewers. This cocktail has a frothy texture and mimics the sweet, savory flavor of the popular snack.

- 2 ounces Sweet Potato–Infused Soju (recipe follows)
- 1 ounce Roasted Sesame Milk (recipe follows)
- 1 ounce Ganjang Syrup (page 130)
- Garnish: roasted sweet potato sprinkled with black sesame seeds

Combine all the ingredients, except the garnish, in a shaking tin with ice. Shake vigorously and then strain into a ceramic mug. Garnish with skewered roasted sweet potato sprinkled with black sesame seeds.

continues →

LUCKY RICE

SERVES 1

This is a cocktail specifically inspired by the New Year's holiday, Seollal, which is celebrated for three days around the end of January. This is a time for families to get together and pay their respects to their ancestors. Families typically enjoy dduk guk, which is a traditional rice cake soup. The oval-shaped rice cakes, which resemble coins, symbolize prosperity, while their white color signifies a fresh start and cleansing upon eating.

- 1¾ ounces Old Forester 100 bourbon or preferred bourbon
- 1 ounce Màkku makgeolli
- ½ ounce Licor 43
- 1½ ounces Toasted Rice Cake Orgeat (recipe follows)
- Garnish: Korean rice cakes

Combine all the ingredients, except the garnish, in a shaking tin with ice. Shake and strain into a brushed metal rice bowl with a large ice cube. Garnish with rice cakes.

TOASTED RICE CAKE ORGEAT

MAKES 3 CUPS

- Equipment: high-speed blender
- 1 cup water
- 50 grams Korean white rice cakes (can be purchased online)
- 1 tea bag Harney & Sons Genmaicha
- 1 cinnamon stick, broken into pieces
- 1 cup Simple Syrup (page 32)
- ½ cup almond milk

Combine the water and rice cakes in a medium pot and cook at a low boil for 10 minutes, or until pillowy soft. Remove from the heat and add the genmaicha tea bag and cinnamon sticks. Steep until it comes to room temperature, approximately an hour. Extract and discard the tea bag. Blend in a high-speed blender until smooth. Strain through cheesecloth into a bowl (should make 1½ cups rice water). Combine the simple syrup and almond milk with the rice water and store in a container in the refrigerator for up to 2 weeks.

RED MONKEY

SERVES 1

One of my greatest joys is discovering a new spirit or an unexpected variation on a familiar one. Sulseam Red Monkey makgeolli was one of those revelations. From the first sip, my synapses lit up with ideas for pairings. Red Monkey is crafted with red yeast rice, giving it a brilliant red hue and a rounder, more full-bodied profile than its classic white counterpart. The red yeast brings out notes of strawberry, raspberry, and dried rose petals. Red Monkey makgeolli is great to pair with such desserts as bingsoo. This cocktail picks up where Red Monkey leaves off, layering in plum, strawberry, toasty rice, and barley. Hopefully, it sparks your senses just as much as it did mine.

1 ounce Sulseam Red Monkey makgeolli

1 ounce Mizu Saga barley shochu

½ ounce The Han Won Mae plum liqueur

½ ounce Toasted Rice Orgeat (recipe follows)

½ ounce Umeboshi Syrup (page 178)

Garnish: 1 Firestix edible flower (optional)

Combine all the ingredients, except the garnish, in a shaking tin filled with ice. Shake until well chilled and double strain into a rocks glass with crushed ice. Top with extra crushed ice and form into a mound. Garnish with Firestix, if desired.

TOASTED RICE ORGEAT

MAKES 2¾ CUPS

Equipment: high-speed blender

1 cup uncooked white rice

1 cup water

1½ cups Simple Syrup (page 32)

2 to 3 cinnamon sticks, crushed

Toast the rice in a pan over medium heat until lightly browned, 1 to 2 minutes. Add all the ingredients to a high-speed blender and blend until totally smooth. Strain through a cheesecloth-lined fine-mesh strainer and store in the refrigerator for up to a month. Give the bottle a shake before using as particles will settle.

DALGONA

SERVES 1

Dalgona coffee is a hugely popular coffee drink in Korea, my spiked version of which is a fun alternative to your usual espresso martini. This is another cocktail that I created for a Netflix collaboration inspired by the K-drama *Squid Game*. In the first season, one of the challenges involves carving out a shape from a dalgona candy, which is the inspiration for the coffee version. Don't worry—no deadly consequences if you fail this challenge!

- 1½ ounces Planteray 3 Stars rum or preferred white rum
- ¾ ounce Frangelico
- ½ ounce coconut soju
- 2 ounces oat milk
- ½ ounce honey syrup (1:1 honey to water)
- Top: 2 large dollops Whipped Korean Coffee (recipe follows)

Combine all the ingredients, except the whipped coffee, in a shaking tin. Shake vigorously, strain into a snifter filled with ice, and spoon the whipped coffee on top.

WHIPPED KOREAN COFFEE

MAKES ½ CUP WHIPPED CREAM

- Equipment: handheld mixer
- ¼ cup instant coffee, such as Maxim
- ¼ cup boiling water
- ¼ cup sugar

Combine all the ingredients in a medium bowl. Whip together, using a handheld mixer, until light and fluffy, with medium-stiff peaks. Store in a container in the refrigerator until ready to use, for up to 1 day.

BANANA KICK

MAKES 1

This cocktail utilizes a childhood favorite of many Koreans—banana milk. Although fresh banana just does not appeal to me texturally, I totally love a synthetic banana flavor. Give me a banana Runt and give me banana milk any day. Banana milk is pure nostalgia to me now, but here, it finds new life in this cocktail.

1 ounce makgeolli

¾ ounce Bori-Cha–Infused Soju (recipe follows)

¼ ounce Jamaican pot still rum

¼ ounce Meletti Amaro liqueur

¼ ounce Giffard Banane du Brésil liqueur

1 barspoon Citric-Malic Solution (page 32)

1¼ ounces Banana Milk Blend (recipe follows)

Garnish: 1 banana leaf and freshly grated nutmeg

Combine all the ingredients, except the garnishes, in a shaking tin filled with ice. Shake vigorously and double strain into a metal cup. Top with crushed ice and shape the ice with your hand like a snow cone. Garnish with a geometrically cut banana leaf and grated nutmeg on top.

continues →

BORI-CHA-INFUSED SOJU

MAKES 2 CUPS

- 2 cups Golden Barley Black Label 40 soju
- 7½ grams Bori-Cha barley drink

Combine the ingredients in a container. Allow to steep for 4 hours minimum. Strain into a bottle and store in a cool, dry place for up to a month.

BANANA MILK BLEND

MAKES 1½ CUPS

- 1 cup Bbingrae banana milk
- ½ cup heavy cream

Combine the ingredients in a quart-size container and top with a lid. Shake three or four times to mix. Allow the liquid to settle, in the refrigerator, for 5 minutes before using. Store in the refrigerator for up to a week.

SOBORO

SERVES 1

If you have ever stepped into a Korean bakery, you have seen these tasty pastry snacks. Soboro are a simple enough pastry—a sweet, pillowy bun characterized by a crumbled, streusel-like topping made of peanuts and sometimes filled with a red bean paste called paht. This cocktail is an homage to the snack, as it gives you the flavor of peanuts and milk bread and paht.

This cocktail utilizes a technique called fat-washing. In this case, browned butter is the fat, which is added to rum and then left in the freezer for several hours. The butter solidifies, but the alcohol does not. The fat can be strained out, leaving the flavor and the texture behind, minus any greasiness or oiliness.

- 1¼ ounces Brown Butter–Washed Rum (recipe follows)
- 1½ ounces Sejong peanut makgeolli
- ¾ ounce Yakju 14 makgeolli
- 1 ounce Paht Syrup (recipe follows)

Combine all the ingredients in a shaking tin filled with ice. Shake until well chilled and strain into a Nick & Nora glass.

continues →

BROWN BUTTER–WASHED RUM

MAKES 2 CUPS

- 1 stick (½ cup) unsalted butter, at room temperature
- 1 cup Ten to One white rum
- 2 teaspoons pure vanilla extract

Place the butter in a small saucepan and place over medium heat. This will ensure the butter browns evenly. The process should take around 7 minutes. Keep a watchful eye on the pan around the 5-minute mark. You should see the milk solids toast and smell nutty. Once the butter is browned, remove from the heat and strain through a cheesecloth-lined chinois.

Transfer the strained butter to a container and combine with the rum and vanilla. Swirl the mixture and allow to mingle for 30 minutes at room temperature. Place in the freezer for a minimum of 24 hours.

After 24 hours, the butter should have solidified into a puck. Using a spoon, break into the layer of butter and remove the puck. Strain the liquid into a bottle. Store in a cool, dry place for up to a month.

NOTE: No need to waste this butter! It can be used in desserts, such as cookies and brownies.

PAHT SYRUP

MAKES 1½ CUPS

- 1 cup paht (smooth red bean paste; can be found online)
- ¾ cup hot water
- ¾ cup Simple Syrup (page 32)

Combine all the ingredients in a container and mix lightly with a spatula. Let steep for 2 hours, or until flavor is incorporated, then strain out the solids. Keep refrigerated for up to a week.

KAKAO TAXI

SERVES 1

Enter my version of the famous soufflé, or lift, cocktail that takes a notorious amount of time and labor to make. The multistep process with elongated shaking is enough to bring down even the fastest, most efficient bartender. I have ordered it at bars before and we know what happens—espresso martini effect! One person sees it being ordered and then everyone around wants one, too. I think it makes so much more sense to make it at home, if you just know the technique and have the time, and you can make it for a limited number of people. Here, the flavors of Korean pear and amaretto work together to create a creamy, soufflélike drink. The name is a play on the style of cocktail called a "lift" and the rideshare app Lyft—Kakao Taxi is a Korean rideshare app.

1½ ounces Sonbi gin

½ ounce Chum Churum or other apple soju

½ ounce Caffo Amaretto

1 ounce Korean pear juice (store-bought or homemade)

¾ ounce heavy cream

¼ ounce freshly squeezed lemon juice

1 egg white

1 ounce chilled club soda, plus more for topping

Combine all the ingredients, except the club soda, in a shaking tin. Add two extra-large ice cubes and shake until extremely chilled, about 30 seconds. Strain into another shaking tin and dry shake vigorously until superfoamy and creamy.

To finish, pour the club soda into a well-chilled collins glass. Pour the cocktail from the mixing tin into the same glass. Once the glass is filled, place it in the freezer to chill for 1 minute. The time allows the foam and the liquid to separate, and the cold temperature helps stiffen the foam. Remove the glass from the freezer and slowly pour more club soda into the center of the foam, from about 5 inches above the glass. The foam should start to rise above the glass. Stop when the foam is an inch or two above the glass. Serve with a straw.

SUIT & CHAI

SERVES 1

I love enjoying cocktails when it's their season to shine. That's not to say I won't sip on a margarita in winter or indulge in a hot cocktail during summer. But there's something special about aligning flavors with the season—such as savoring a chai-inspired cocktail on a crisp autumn day. Enter Suit & Chai, a cocktail I created for a Ssam Bar autumn lineup. The first sip hits you with the rich, nutty creaminess of salted chestnut, followed by a refreshing, fizzy finish of crisp autumn flavors. McCol Barley soda is a Korean soft drink that tastes like Coca-Cola steeped in cereal grains and can be found at your local Korean grocery or H-Mart.

- 2 ounces Chai-Infused Rum (recipe follows)
- ½ ounce Rockey's Liqueur
- ½ ounce Ginseng Cordial (page 69)
- ¼ ounce Citric-Malic Solution (page 32)
- 2 ounces McCol carbonated barley drink, or Chinotto Italian soda
- Top: large dollop Salted Chestnut Makgeolli Cream (recipe follows) plus ground cinnamon

Combine all the ingredients, except the cream and cinnamon, in a shaking tin with ice. Shake and strain into a tall glass over ice. Gently top with Chestnut Makgeolli Cream and sprinkle with ground cinnamon.

continues →

5

SPIRIT FORWARD

강한 증류주

GANJANG OLD-FASHIONED

SERVES 1

When ganjang is added to brown sugar and water, the effect is akin to a rich, salted caramel. Old-fashioneds can sometimes lean too sweet, so the ganjang adds a savory depth that balances the drink. This syrup isn't just for cocktails—it's also fantastic drizzled over vanilla ice cream or in your coffee.

2 ounces Old Forester 100 bourbon or preferred bourbon

½ ounce Ganjang Syrup (recipe follows)

3 dashes Angostura bitters

3 dashes Angostura orange bitters

Garnish: 1 orange peel

Combine all the ingredients, except the garnish, in a mixing glass and stir with a barspoon. Strain into a rocks glass with a large cube and garnish with an expressed orange peel.

GANJANG SYRUP

MAKES 2¼ CUPS

Equipment: blender

16 ounces dark brown sugar

2 cups water

2 tablespoons Sempio ganjang (or your favorite soy sauce)

Place all the ingredients in a blender and start blending at low speed. Increase the speed steadily to high until the ingredients become fully incorporated. Store in the refrigerator for up to a month.

JEJU ORANGE CHOCOLATE

SERVES 1

The Jeju Orange chocolate is a popular sweet treat from the island and is made with Hallabong, a premium citrus variety known for its sweet, tangy flavor and fragrant aroma, thanks to Jeju's volcanic soil and subtropical climate. Ninome tangerine soju is a unique soju from Jeju, which blends rice, volcanic rock water, and locally grown, sun-dried tangerine peels. In this cocktail, crème de cacao adds the final touch to re-create the flavor profile of the popular confection.

1½ ounces bourbon

1 ounce Ninome tangerine soju

½ ounce Tempus Fugit crème de cacao

1 ounce Orange Oleo Saccharum (recipe follows)

Garnish: 1 square Jeju Orange chocolate, or 1 chocolate mushroom

Combine all the ingredients, except the garnish, in a mixing glass filled with ice. Stir with a barspoon until well chilled and then pour into a rocks glass over a large ice cube. Garnish with a Jeju Chocolate Orange square or a chocolate mushroom, if easier to procure.

ORANGE OLEO SACCHARUM

MAKES 1½ CUPS

Equipment: citrus juicer, high-speed blender

4 large oranges, or enough to yield 250 grams of juice

250 grams sugar

Peel the oranges with a citrus peeler and set aside 50 grams of the peel. Juice all the oranges to get 250 grams of juice. Combine the orange juice and sugar in a high-speed blender without turning on the blender. Add the reserved orange peels and turn the blender on for 1 minute, or until sugar and peels are completely dissolved. Strain through a fine-mesh strainer into a container and store in the refrigerator for up to 2 weeks.

ODUM OF NIGHT

SERVES 1

A brooding cocktail for the contemplative drinker (think: stoic businessman in a K-drama), this one's for those who appreciate a whiskey cocktail with depth and nuance. Ki One brings a spicy, malted backbone, while white soy brings a subtle umami savoriness that rounds out the slightly bitter, slightly sweet, and ultimately sippable profile. Bacchus-D is a noncarbonated energy drink chock-full of vitamins, which is having its own "Red Bull and vodka" moment in Korea. It has a flavor akin to sour candy and lends a nice tangy dimension to this late-night concoction.

1½ ounces Ki One Batch 1 Virgin American Oak single malt Korean whisky

½ ounce Jujube-Infused Sweet Vermouth (page 148)

½ ounce Diplomatico rum

½ ounce Bacchus-D

¼ ounce white soy sauce

4 drops Mugwort Citrus Bitters (recipe follows)

Garnish: 1 kinome leaf (edible young Japanese Sancho pepper leaf, available online and at specialty stores)

Combine all the ingredients, except the garnish, in a mixing glass with ice. Stir with a barspoon until chilled, then double strain into a single rocks glass with a large ice cube. Garnish with the kinome leaf.

continues →

SOHAN NEGRONI

SERVES 1

Earthy, slightly bitter, sweet, fruity. This cocktail is everything you want to sip on while waiting for your banchan to arrive. It is a less bitter take on a Negroni, crafted specifically to suit the Korean palate. Koreans haven't historically been inclined to bitter cocktails, mostly enjoying refreshing, sweet cocktails. Of course, palates have changed and many classic cocktails are very familiar now. This one is a perfect bridge for those who want to take the leap. Dried persimmons taste similar to figs and they add a molasses-like, seasonal element when steeped in sweet vermouth. "Sohan" refers to the coldest time of the year on the Lunar Calendar.

1 ounce Hyeonmi-Infused Gin (recipe follows)

1 ounce Jujube-Infused Sweet Vermouth (recipe follows)

¾ ounce Campari

¼ ounce Yangchon chungju

Garnish: 1 orange peel

Combine all the ingredients, excpt the garnish, in a mixing glass with ice. Stir with a barspoon until well chilled. Strain into a rocks glass with a large ice cube. Cut out a coin from an orange peel and express it. Garnish on top of the ice cube.

continues →

MARTINI ROYALE

JINOO KO, BAR DIRECTOR AT OIJI MI, NEW YORK

SERVES 1

Samhae soju has the distinct honor of being recognized as an "Intangible Cultural Heritage" by the city of Seoul, as it is brewed from only rice, nuruk, and water, using a 300-year-old recipe handed down for generations. It undergoes a slow fermentation spanning three months. Jinoo Ko shares, "Samhae soju packs a punch with huge savory mushroom-y tasting notes. As a counterpart of the Samhae soju, I used Damsoul soju, made by brewing the rice with spruce and pine needles, then distilled and proofed down with spruce tea. This particular soju carries this bright, refreshing, and yet resinous quality when diluted. Pairing these very different sojus created a unique and aromatic soju martini supported by the classic vermouth, Dolin dry."

1½ ounces Samhae soju

1 ounce Solsongju Damsoul pine soju

½ ounce Dolin dry vermouth

Garnish: 1 huge lemon twist, and (optional) golden Kaluga caviar

Combine all the ingredients, except the garnishes, in a mixing glass with ice and stir with a barspoon. Stir for a long time until almost double in volume through dilution. Strain into a coupe glass and express a huge twist of lemon to garnish. Optional: Garnish a quenelle of Kaluga caviar in a spoon on the side.

SOUTHSIDE BREAKFAST

ROY KIM, OWNER-BARTENDER AT POMME BAR, SEOUL

SERVES 1

This cocktail is inspired by a typical Korean breakfast of miso soup and coffee, reimagined as a cocktail. Here, miso is panfried with Korean mint and coffee to create a unique drink. Roy Kim states, "You can enjoy the savory flavor of miso and the rich taste of coffee at the same time."

1¾ ounces Breakfast Whiskey (recipe follows)

¼ ounce Coffee Syrup (recipe follows)

Garnishes: 1 Korean mint (bang-a) leaf and 2 coffee beans

Combine all the ingredients, except the garnishes, in a mixing glass and stir well. Strain into a rocks glass with a large ice cube and garnish with the Korean mint leaf and two coffee beans.

continues →

NURUK WHISKY

MAKES 2 CUPS

1 cup Dewar's White Scotch
1 cup plus 6 tablespoons water
28 grams nuruk powder (available online)
27 grams Hishiroku white koji (available online)
16 grams loose barley tea
32 grams sugar
1½ grams citric acid

Put everything into a resealable plastic bag and seal with as little air as possible. Leave overnight at room temperature. Strain twice through a coffee filter into a container. Store in a cool, dry place for up to 2 weeks.

NURUK CARBONATED WATER

MAKES 2 CUPS

Equipment: soda siphon, 2 CO_2 cartridges
2 cups water
120 grams nuruk powder

Combine the ingredients in a resealable plastic bag and seal with as little air as possible. Leave overnight at room temperature. Strain twice with a coffee filter to remove the solids. Add the liquid to a soda siphon and charge with two CO_2 cartridges.

ELYSIUM

CHARLIE KIM, BAR MANAGER AT MO BAR, SEOUL

SERVES 1

Mo Bar, located in the Mandarin Oriental in Seoul, is lauded for its approach to minimal wastage. This sustainable and delicious cocktail was created to repurpose leftover wine from the bar and leftover bread from breakfast at the restaurant next door.

1¼ ounces Sustainable Carbohydrate Vermouth (recipe follows)

1 ounce Tokki Soju Black

¾ ounce Hwayo 25 soju

0.2 ounce (or 1 barspoon) aloe vera juice

Garnish: 1 lemon peel

Combine all the ingredients, except the lemon peel, in a shaking tin and shake with ice. Double strain into a martini glass and express a small piece of lemon peel.

SUSTAINABLE CARBOHYDRATE VERMOUTH

MAKES 2 CUPS

100 grams stale bread

2 cups leftover white wine

1 gram whole cloves

1 star anise pod

1¾ ounces vodka

Break up the stale bread into smaller pieces. Heat the wine in a nonreactive medium saucepan over low heat. Add the bread, cloves, and star anise and reduce by 20 percent. Strain out the solids, add the vodka, bottle, and store in the refrigerator for up to 3 weeks.

NOTE: This handcrafted vermouth can be a great modifier for a martini. Follow the usual specs and swap out the dry vermouth.

6

SAVORY & SPICY

짭짤하고 매콤한

TRAIN TO BUSAN

SERVES 1

At the time of its release in 2016, this zombie flick set box office records in Korea. I had to name my spin on a Zombie cocktail after this film. The classic Zombie cocktail was created by the legendary Donn Beach in the 1930s. This cocktail is known for being superboozy, with a blend of rums, falernum, and grapefruit. My version replaces falernum with orgeat, but the rums are present, and the addition of Jinro grapefruit soju gives this a more citrusy vibe. The gochujang orgeat gives the cocktail a touch of heat and savoriness, which I think just makes you keep wanting to go back for more.

- 1 ounce Jinro or other grapefruit soju
- 1 ounce Ten to One white rum
- ½ ounce Smith & Cross Jamaican rum
- ½ ounce Copalli cacao rum
- 1 ounce freshly squeezed grapefruit juice
- ½ ounce freshly squeezed lime juice
- 1 ounce Gochujang Apple Orgeat (recipe follows)
- Garnish: Pineapple fronds, a grapefruit wheel, or whatever else you want to add—tiki drinks are meant to be over the top!

Combine all the ingredients, except the garnish, in a shaking tin filled with ice. Shake vigorously and pour into a ceramic or tiki mug. Add your choice of garnishes.

GOCHUJANG APPLE ORGEAT

MAKES 1½ CUPS

- Equipment: high-speed blender
- 1 cup Giffard orgeat
- 3 ounces apple cider
- 1½ teaspoons gochujang

Combine all the ingredients in a blender. Blend until fully smooth and store in a container in the refrigerator for up to a month. Shake the bottle before using, as particles will settle.

GAMTAE MARTINI

SERVES 1

Gamtae is a rare and special variety of gim (seaweed), which can only be found in the southern coastal waters of Korea. It grows naturally in clean seawater and cannot be farmed, making it challenging to source. Gamtae's distinctive flavor profile is marked by deep salinity, rich umami, and truffle. It adds a remarkable flavor to a savory-leaning martini. The kombu in this martini adds a silky texture. Enjoyed with nibbles of the crunchy garnish, this cocktail is the perfect aperitif.

- 1½ ounces Gamtae-Kombu Gin (recipe follows)
- 1 ounce Pungjeong Sagye Winter 42 soju
- ¾ ounce Dolin dry vermouth
- ¼ ounce dry sake
- Garnish: 1 piece Crispy Gim (recipe follows)

Combine all the ingredients, except the garnish, in a mixing glass with ice. Stir with a barspoon until well chilled. Double strain into a martini glass and garnish with a Crispy Gim on top.

continues →

LAPSANG-INFUSED SHERRY

MAKES 1 CUP

- 1 cup Lustau East India Sherry
- 5 grams Lapsang Souchong tea

Combine the ingredients in a container. Steep for 4 hours at room temperature. Strain and store in the refrigerator.

SHIITAKE-INFUSED SOJU

MAKES 375 MILLILITERS

- One 375-milliliter bottle Chum Churum soju or preferred plain soju
- 12 grams dried shiitake mushrooms
- 12 grams shredded carrot

Combine all the ingredients in a container. Steep for 24 hours in the refrigerator, strain, and store in the refrigerator for up to 2 weeks.

NABAK SOJU

SERVES 1

This savory soju cocktail features nabak kimchi broth, which is enjoyed for being mild, refreshing, and slightly fizzy. It is the simplest form of cabbage kimchi, but it sure does pack a punch! It's also perfect for those who don't want anything spicy. Topped with Sprite or 7UP, it turns sweet, tangy, and savory in all the right ways. Trust me, it works!

3 ounces Nabak Kimchi (recipe follows)

2 ounces Jinro 24 soju

2 ounces Sprite or 7UP

Garnish: Nabak Kimchi (recipe follows)

Combine all the ingredients, except the garnish, in a small metal bowl with a large ice cube. Garnish with kimchi pieces on top.

NABAK KIMCHI

MAKES 2 QUARTS

1 pound napa cabbage

1 tablespoon Korean sea salt, divided in half

3½ cups warm water

2 tablespoons Sprite or 7UP

1 tablespoon roughly chopped garlic

½ cup chopped red chile pepper, chopped

2 green onions, chopped roughly

Gather napa cabbage leaves of similar size, stack them up, and cut them lengthwise, then make square-shaped (nabak) cuts, approximately 4 inches in size. Toss in 1½ teaspoons of the salt and set aside. After an hour, wash the cabbage leaves and squeeze them dry.

Combine the warm water, Sprite, chopped garlic, and the remaining 1½ teaspoons of salt in a large bowl. Stir quickly until the salt is all dissolved. Add the red chile pepper and green onions to the bowl, along with the cabbage. Pour the warm salt water from above onto the cabbage. Cover the container and store it in a cool, dry place for 48 to 72 hours. After 72 hours, store in the refrigerator.

CHICKEN MOO MARTINI

SERVES 1

I assure you, no chickens or cows will be harmed in the making of this cocktail. "Chicken Moo" is a slang term for the white pickled radish cubes that come with an order of Korean fried chicken, which would never be complete without this accompaniment to cleanse your palate after every bite of chicken. You will also find that once the radishes are gone, you are left with a sweet, tangy, savory brine that I proudly admit to having drunk from its container. In this case, we can be more civilized and make it into a martini that stands up to any dirty martini.

- 1½ ounces Solsongju Damsoul pine soju
- 1 ounce vodka
- ½ ounce Yangchon chungju
- 1 ounce Chicken Moo brine (recipe follows, or use store-bought)
- Garnish: 6 to 7 drops Scallion Oil and Chicken Moo brine (recipes follow)

Combine all the ingredients, except the garnishes, in a shaking tin, add ice, and shake vigorously. Strain into a martini or Nick & Nora glass. Garnish with Scallion Oil and a side of skewered Chicken Moo.

continues →

CHICKEN MOO

MAKES 2 CUPS

- 2 cups 1-inch-cubed daikon radish
- 1 cup water
- ¾ cup distilled white vinegar
- ½ cup sugar
- 1 tablespoon kosher salt

Place the daikon in a quart-size container. Add the rest of the ingredients, seal, and leave in the refrigerator to pickle for a minimum of 24 hours. Store in the refrigerator for up to 2 weeks.

SCALLION OIL

MAKES ⅓ CUP

- Equipment: high-speed blender
- 3 cups water
- 4 scallions
- ⅓ cup neutral oil

Bring the water to a boil. Meanwhile, cut the green parts of 4 scallions in 4-inch pieces. The white parts can be reserved for any future cooking. Prepare an ice bath. Boil the green scallion tops for 30 seconds, then drain and transfer to the ice bath for 15 seconds.

In a high-speed blender, process the scallions with the oil until smooth, then strain through a cheesecloth-lined strainer. Transfer the scallion oil to an eyedropper bottle and refrigerate for up to 2 weeks.

PB&J

SERVES 1

All-American staple meets Korean (and some Japanese) influence in a cocktail format. Here's how: Bokbunja plays the role of the jelly, which floats on top of the cocktail. When you take a sip, the jelly hits you first and then the peanut butter kicks in, giving the effect of biting into a PB&J. The peanut butter rum uses a simple fat-washing technique of extracting the flavor of peanut butter and infusing it with the alcohol.

2 ounces Peanut Butter–Washed Rum (recipe follows)
½ ounce Jeju Udo peanut makgeolli
½ ounce Umeboshi Syrup (recipe follows)
½ ounce Citric-Malic Solution (page 32)
Float: bokbunja

Combine all the ingredients, except the bokbunja, in a shaking tin filled with ice. Shake and strain into a double rocks glass over a large ice cube. Float the bokbunja by placing the back of a barspoon over top of the glass and pouring slowly. Allow it to gently layer on top without mixing.

continues →

PEANUT BUTTER–WASHED RUM

MAKES 2 CUPS

- 500 grams creamy peanut butter
- 2 cups Planteray 3 Stars rum or preferred white rum

Spread the peanut butter in a thin, even layer on the bottom of a loaf pan. Pour the rum on top, but do not mix. Cover the pan and let it sit at room temperature for 24 hours. Place in the freezer for 1 hour, to allow the peanut butter to harden. Strain the liquid through a cheesecloth-lined chinois into a bottle and store in a cool, dry place for up to 2 weeks.

UMEBOSHI SYRUP

MAKES 3 CUPS

- 500 grams water
- 350 grams sugar
- 65 grams umeboshi paste

Boil the water. Combine the hot water and the rest of the ingredients in a quart-size heatproof container and mix until fully incorporated. Allow to fully cool before ready to use. Store in the refrigerator for up to a month.

Kloud
Premium Lager
100 %
OG
100 %
Alc. 5% Vol.

KIMCHI MICHELADA

SERVES 1

Kimchi juice is liquid gold. It is tangy, funky, umami-rich, and spicy, not to mention chock-full of antioxidants and probiotics. It can have different applications depending on the fermentation levels, and these levels are constantly evolving. The oldest, funkiest, gone-too-sour kimchi can be the most incredible base for soup or added to batter for kimchi pancakes. This Michelada benefits from just-sour to borderline too-funky kimchi juice. A little goes a long way, and the resulting flavor is so savory and delicious.

One 12-ounce Korean beer, such as Terra or Kloud

Tajín for rimming

1 ounce Yangchon chungju

3 ounces Kimchi Michelada Mix (recipe follows)

Garnish: 1 celery stick and 1 pickled pepper

Open a can of beer with a smooth-edged peer can opener (found online) and pour it into a pint-size container. Rim the beer can with Tajín and add the chungju and Kimchi Michelada Mix. Top with the beer and garnish with the celery stick and pickled pepper, or anything else you desire.

KIMCHI MICHELADA MIX

MAKES 2½ CUPS

2 cups Clamato juice

½ cup kimchi juice

2 ounces freshly squeezed lemon juice

1 teaspoon gochujang

1 teaspoon oligo yeot

Mix together all the ingredients in a container or pitcher. Store in the refrigerator for up to 2 weeks.

K-MARGARITA

SERVES 1

This cocktail was inspired by my love of a spicy margarita. This one utilizes Korean chili peppers, which I grew up eating simply dipped in gochujang. The chili pepper brings a little heat and a fruity flavor to the tequila infusion, while the interplay of yuja honey and kalamansi is a playful twist on the traditional lime. To complete the profile of this addicting snack, rim the glass with gochugaru and sea salt.

- Fine gochugaru powder, for rimming
- 2 ounces Korean Chile Pepper–Infused Tequila (recipe follows)
- ½ ounce Xila Licor de Agave
- 1 ounce kalamansi puree
- ¾ ounce Spicy Yuja Honey (page 113)
- Garnish: 1 lime wedge

Rim a double rocks glass with gochugaru powder. Build the cocktail in a shaking tin filled with ice. Shake vigorously and strain into the glass filled with ice. Garnish with the lime wedge.

KOREAN CHILE PEPPER-INFUSED TEQUILA

MAKES 2 CUPS

- 75 grams Korean green chile pepper, chopped (remove stem, but keep ribs and seeds)
- 2 cups Casco Viejo tequila blanco

Steep together ingredients at room temperature for at least 24 hours. You can even steep the peppers indefinitely. Store the container in the refrigerator for up to a month.

BOATFIRE GIMLET

BENJAMIN HOPKINS, BEVERAGE DIRECTOR AT PITT'S, BROOKLYN

SERVES 1

Ben Hopkins and I have worked together on pop-ups in New York that featured Korean ingredients. When they set out to create a spicy drink that complemented the huge flavors of sotol, Ben states, "I wanted to make sure to contour the bigger flavors, and anchovy sauce did exactly that. It's like a mega-saline."

1¼ ounces Cardenxe Sotol

¾ ounce Morita and Long Pepper–Infused Mezcal (recipe follows)

¾ ounce freshly squeezed lime juice

¾ ounce agave syrup (1:1 agave to water)

¼ teaspoon myeolchi aekjot (Korean anchovy sauce)

Garnish: 1 shrimp chip

Build the drink in a shaking tin, shake, and double strain into a Nick & Nora glass. Garnish with a skewered shrimp chip.

MORITA AND LONG PEPPER–INFUSED MEZCAL

750 MILLILITERS

750 milliliters Espadín mezcal

1 large ripe Morita chile

1 Korean long pepper

2 large shallots, diced

Combine all the ingredients in a large, nonreactive container, cover, and let infuse for 24 hours. After 24 hours, strain away the solids thoroughly and store the infused mezcal in a bottle in the refrigerator for up to a month.

NOTE: A full-bottle infusion is great for use in a spicy mezcal margarita.

CHUNGJU GIMBAP

DONGJUN CHOI, OWNER AND BARTENDER OF BAR CHAM, SEOUL

SERVES 1

Owner Dongjun Choi explains a favorite drink on Bar Cham's menu: "We've reimagined gimbap, one of Korea's iconic dishes, in the form of a cocktail. Using soju made from rice—specifically, Tokki Black from Chungju—and makgeolli as the base, this drink captures the essence of gimbap with notes of cucumber, sesame oil, and a subtle kick of wasabi."

1½ ounces Tokki Soju Black
½ ounce Makgeolli Wasabi Shrub (recipe follows)
¾ ounce cucumber juice
½ ounce freshly squeezed lemon juice
¼ ounce Simple Syrup (page 32)
2 drops toasted sesame oil
Garnish: Black sesame seeds

Combine all the ingredients, except the garnish, in a shaking tin, shake vigorously, and strain into a black ceramic mug. Garnish with a pinch of black sesame seeds in the center.

MAKGEOLLI WASABI SHRUB

MAKES ½ CUP

Equipment: blender
2 tablespoons makgeolli
1 tablespoon white wine vinegar
45 grams sugar
1½ grams wasabi powder

Combine all the ingredients in a blender, blend lightly, then strain through a fine-mesh colander, bottle, and store in the refrigerator.

MIYEOK MARTINI

GREGORY KONG, BAR DIRECTOR AT NOMAD TEA PARLOR, NEW YORK

SERVES 1

Greg Kong is often inspired by food and meals he has eaten. Describing this cocktail, he says, "I had recently enjoyed some miyeok guk (seaweed soup) and wanted to come up with a drink that incorporated seaweed as the briny element to make a 'dirty' martini. The 'aha' moment for me was trying the Yangchon chungju for the first time. It has some wonderfully complex savory and umami notes to it that really helped balance the seaweed flavor and bring all of the elements together."

1½ ounces Seaweed-Infused Gin (recipe follows)
½ ounce Yangchon chungju
½ ounce dry riesling
½ teaspoon Tomato Water (recipe follows)
2 dashes Black Pepper Tincture (recipe follows)
Garnish: 3 small drops toasted sesame oil

Combine all the ingredients, except the garnish, in a mixing glass filled with ice. Stir with a barspoon until well chilled. Strain into a Nick & Nora glass and garnish with three small drops of toasted sesame oil.

continues →

SEAWEED-INFUSED GIN

MAKES 1 CUP

1 cup Gray Whale gin

4 grams miyeok (can be found online)

Combine the gin and miyeok in a container and let sit for 4 hours at room temperature. Strain through a coffee filter and store in the refrigerator for up to 2 weeks.

TOMATO WATER

MAKES ¼ CUP

Equipment: blender

1 large tomato (roughly 200 grams)

1 gram kosher salt

Cut the tomato in chunks and place in a blender along with the salt. Blend on high speed until pureed. Place tomato pulp in a cheesecloth-lined strainer and let the tomato water drip into a glass bowl or other nonreactive container. Do not stir, mix, or otherwise agitate. Put in the refrigerator and let drip overnight. Tomato water will keep for 2 to 3 days in the refrigerator.

BLACK PEPPER TINCTURE

MAKES ½ CUP

15 grams whole black peppercorns

4 ounces Everclear (or other high-proof spirit)

¾ ounce water

Crush the peppercorns until they are roughly broken up. Combine the black pepper and Everclear in a glass jar and seal. Let sit at room temperature for 48 hours. Strain through a coffee filter, add the water to strained tincture, and store in an eyedropper bottle in a cool, dry place for up to 2 weeks.

NAENGMYUN MARTINI

SARAH KU, BAR DIRECTOR AT KIMCHI48 AND GOLDENHOF, NEW YORK

SERVES 1

Sarah Ku states, "My inspiration behind this cocktail mostly stems from how I like to build most of my menus and drinks: How can I re-create a flavor or feeling while I'm drinking? I truly wanted to capture all the savory notes of one of my favorite Korean dishes, as I used to have it almost twice or three times a week in between my doubles during summer at a nearby food hall in K-Town. Part of me also wanted to lean in to the joke of making a 'soup'-tail as well. A dirty gin martini drinker, to me, looks for the same thing as I do when I'm ordering a naengmyun: a very very, very cold first sip; a rounded lush flavor from the brine; and a floral brightness whether from the gin or from mustard oil. It was a no-brainer at that point; just approach the cocktail with the same philosophy as the perfect dirty vodka martini."

- 2½ ounces Sesame Gin (recipe follows)
- ¾ ounce Naengmyun Broth (recipe follows)
- Rinse: Dolin dry vermouth
- Garnish: 1 cucumber ribbon

Combine the cocktail ingredients, except the rinse and garnish, in a stirring tin, add ice, and stir. Pour into a dry vermouth–rinsed coupe. Garnish with a skewered cucumber ribbon.

continues →

7

FROZEN & LARGE FORMAT

냉동 및 대용량

BOKBUNJA SANGRIA

SERVES 4 TO 6

Bokbunja is given the sangria treatment here. The warming spices come from the sujeonggwa syrup, which is made with cinnamon, ginger, and jujube. Sujeonggwa is a traditional chilled drink served in a small cup at the end of a meal, doubling as both a palate cleanser and a sweet treat. This sangria is versatile: enjoy it warm as a mulled wine, or pour it over crushed ice for a refreshing twist.

- One 375-milliliter bottle bokbunja (e.g., Bohae)
- 2 cups pinot noir
- 1 cup Jinro strawberry soju
- ½ cup triple sec
- ½ cup St-Rémy Brandy or preferred brandy
- 1 cup freshly squeezed orange juice
- ½ cup Sujeonggwa Syrup (recipe follows)
- Garnishes: Sliced jujubes and cinnamon sticks (optional)

Combine all the ingredients, except the garnishes, in a large container and whisk until fully incorporated. Pour the batch into a large serving vessel filled with ice. I use a traditional ramen metal pot and serve it with a ladle. Scatter jujubes into the pot over the ice and serve with cinnamon sticks in each cup, if desired.

SUJEONGGWA SYRUP

MAKES 3 CUPS

- 2 cups water
- 16 ounces light brown sugar
- 5 dried jujubes (Chinese red dates), chopped
- 4 cinnamon sticks
- 50 grams fresh ginger, peeled and sliced thinly

Combine all the ingredients in a pot and bring to a simmer over medium heat. Simmer for 10 minutes. Strain out the solids and store the syrup in the refrigerator for up to a month.

JOLLY PONG MILK PUNCH

SERVES 3 OR 4

Jolly Pong is a very popular puffed rice snack that looks like American Honey Smacks, but is nuttier and has a flavor akin to misugaru, a popular Korean drink made from roasted and ground grain powder. There are notes of sesame, barley, brown rice, and red beans. The snack entered the market in 1972 and has remained popular to this day. Oftentimes, it is enjoyed with milk and eaten like a cereal. In this preparation, the cocktail is clarified in steeped Jolly Pong milk. The cocktail also utilizes steeped hyeonmi cha, which is a tea made with roasted brown rice and green tea leaves. The resulting cocktail is mildly nutty, with honey notes.

1 tablespoon, or 1 tea bag, hyeonmi-cha
6 ounces boiling water
8 ounces Jinro 24 soju
2 ounces white rum
2 ounces overproof rum
2 ounces aged brandy (e.g., St-Rémy VSOP)
½ ounce Tempus Fugit crème de moka or Kahlúa coffee liqueur
4 ounces honey
2½ ounces Citric-Malic Solution (page 32)
12 ounces Jolly Pong Milk (recipe follows)
Garnish: 3 or 4 Jolly Pong puffs

Steep the hyeonmi-cha in the boiling water for 5 to 7 minutes. Set aside to cool. Combine all the other ingredients, except the garnish, in a measuring cup. Slowly pour the cocktail mixture into the bowl of strained Jolly Pong Milk. Chill in the refrigerator for 3 to 4 hours, allowing the milk to curdle. Do not disturb the mixture during this time. Then, remove from the fridge and strain through a coffee filter–lined chinois. The first few ounces of liquid will be cloudy, so as soon as the mixture runs clear, swap out the container and add the cloudy liquid back to strain again.

To serve, pour 5 ounces into a brandy snifter over an ice cube, and garnish with three or four Jolly Pong puffs on top of a large ice cube.

JOLLY PONG MILK

MAKES ABOUT 1½ CUPS

12 ounces whole milk
1 cup Jolly Pong puffs

Combine the ingredients in a quart-size container and give it a quick shake. Infuse for 2 hours in the refrigerator, then strain into a large bowl and discard the solids.

KOR-CHATA

SERVES 4

I created this as a variation on horchata, which is a Mexican drink made with rice and cinnamon. My version incorporates Korean Morning Rice Drink, which can be found in Korean grocery stores and, just as the name proclaims, is often enjoyed in the morning for breakfast. According to the brand, it provides a great source of energy, promotes digestive health, and supports a balanced diet. I think it tastes like horchata. Hyeonmi-cha is tea made from roasted short-grain brown rice and adds nuttiness to the overall profile of the cocktail.

Equipment: high-speed blender

¾ cup Probitas white rum

¾ cup makgeolli

½ cup Hyeonmi-Cha–Infused Rye (recipe follows)

1 cup Morning Rice Drink

¼ cup ssal-yeot

1 cinnamon stick, crushed

Garnish: 4 cinnamon sticks

Blend together all the ingredients, except the garnish, in a high-speed blender. Strain through a fine-mesh strainer into a makgeolli teapot. Serve over ice in makgeolli cups and garnish each with a cinnamon stick.

HYEONMI-CHA-INFUSED RYE

MAKES 1 CUP

1 cup Old Overholt straight rye

1 tea bag hyeonmi-cha

Combine the ingredients and allow the tea to steep for 30 minutes. Strain out and discard the tea bag and store the infused rye in a cool, dry place for up to a month.

Live & Active Probiotic
L. paracasei strain Shirota
Yakult

FUN SHOT

SERVES 1

This is a supersimple, but *fun* shot that can be a great option for a dessert at a dinner party or for a large crowd of friends. Yakult is an extremely popular probiotic beverage that is enjoyed by all ages. It has a milky, citrusy, tangy flavor that is like a much lighter, sweeter version of kefir. Like most yogurt-based products, this drink is great for digestion. The active ingredient, lactobacillus, is known for its immune-modulating effect as well. Science aside, Yakult packs a flavor punch. Just check out its serving size—this is called a fun shot for a reason! The soju shot of your choice is followed by a partially frozen, slushified Yakult in its original container. Just puncture it with a straw and enjoy!

1 Yakult
2 ounces soju

Freeze the Yakult and then allow it to unfreeze at room temperature for 15 minutes before serving. The result will be a slushed Yakult, easy to sip from a straw. Serve the soju in a shot glass. If you want a fun presentation, serve the Yakult and soju shot on a mini tray over crushed ice.

BOKBUNJA GRANITA & CHAMPAGNE

SERVES 4

Granita is one of my favorite ways of adding chill to a cocktail—you don't need to add any additional ice! Once the granita is ready, you can just scrape and spoon it into a glass and top with your favorite Champagne or sparkling wine. It is perfect for a summer day, or substitute it for dessert at your next party. The berries and Champagne are an infallible combination, with bokbunja adding an extra punch of dark raspberry flavor to the frozen mixed berries.

Equipment: high-speed blender or food processor

5 ounces water

16 ounces frozen mixed berries

1 cup sugar

2 cups bokbunja

3 ounces Ninome tangerine soju, or Cointreau

1 cup pomegranate juice

½ teaspoon pure vanilla extract

4 or 5 dashes Regan's Orange Bitters

Top (per glass): 3 ounce of your favorite Champagne or sparkling wine

Garnish: Frozen mixed berries

Combine the water, berries, and sugar in a medium pot and simmer over low heat until the sugar dissolves and the berries break down, about 5 minutes. Puree the mixture in a high-speed blender or food processer and then fine-mesh strain into a container, taking time to press the fruit down to extract all the juices. Add the bokbunja, soju, pomegranate juice, vanilla, and bitters and whisk together. Pour the mixture into a 9-inch square cake pan and allow to freeze for around 5 hours, scraping the mixture every 30 to 45 minutes, to introduce ice crystals.

To serve, scoop two generous spoonfuls of the granita into a coupe or martini glass. Top with your favorite Champagne. Garnish with frozen mixed berries.

MELONA SLUSHY

SERVES 2

Melona, the most popular Korean imported frozen dessert on a stick, was created in 1992—a time when honeydew was still an unfamiliar fruit in Korea. Since its debut, the original melon flavor has achieved iconic status both in Korea and abroad. Over time, it has expanded into a lineup of other well-loved flavors, my personal favorite being mango. This slushy cocktail pays tribute to the ice treat by combining two of my favorite flavors into one, the original and the mango.

Equipment: blender

2 ounces Gorae Honey-Do soju

2 ounces Good Day or other mango soju

2 ounces vodka

1 ounce Meloncello liqueur

3 ounces Boiron or The Perfect Purée mango puree

3 ounces Boiron or The Perfect Purée cantaloupe puree

2 ounces Calpico

½ ounce Citric-Malic Solution (page 32)

2½ cups ice

Garnish: 2 mint sprigs

Combine all the ingredients, except the garnish, in a blender and blend on high speed until slushified. Pour into glasses of your choice and top each with a mint sprig.

SOMAEK MULE

SERVES 4

A version of this cocktail was created for a pop-up collaboration with Tokki Soju, featuring their Tokki White expression. Tokki White is especially well suited for cocktails as it has the character to stand up to the bold flavors of ginger beer. The drink itself is a mash-up of two classics: Korean somaek, which is a beloved combination of soju and beer, and a Moscow Mule, a classic highball. Blending these inspirations into a frozen treat results in a completely new flavor profile that pays homage to tradition while offering something refreshingly modern.

1 cup Tokki Soju White

One 12-ounce can ginger beer, such as Bundaberg

One to two 12-ounce cans Korean beer, such as Terra

Garnish: 4 lime wedges (optional)

Fill two standard ice cube trays halfway with Tokki White and then top with ginger beer. Freeze for 24 hours. The ice cubes will remain firm but slightly slushy, due to the alcohol content. Add four or five cubes to each of four glass mugs and top with beer. Garnish with lime wedges, if desired.

Cahors
SHAKE & ENJOY
SINCE 1980
SACSAC
ORANGE
LOTTE
생 배
갈아만든주스
SINCE 1981
Tae Kwon Do
Playing Yut

15
18
SOON
HARI
Active Probiotic

POCHA PARTY PACK!

SERVES 4

At Ssam Bar, we had rooms upstairs with private karaoke, and I was able to create some really fun large-format packs for revelers to enjoy, in a more DIY fashion. Sort of like what you would get in a norebang (Korean karaoke bar), but with a refined look. Here, a hangiri—a traditional round container for sushi rice—is the vessel for this tableside make-your-own-drinks soju presentation.

Three 375-milliliter bottles assorted green bottle soju

2 to 3 bottles Yakult

Assorted bottles of soda, such as Bong and Sac Sac

Lime, lemon, and orange wheels

Crushed ice

Arrange everything over crushed ice, taking care to place items in groups and scattering the garnishes all over for an aesthetic effect. Include shot glasses and regular glasses filled with ice.

SUJEONGGWA

JAE BAE, @JARBAE

SERVES 4

Jae is known for taking well-known flavor combinations or food dishes and brilliantly translating them into drink form. He reflects, "Sujeonggwa is truly a traditional staple of Korean beverages. A spiced and sweet end to any meal, sujeonggwa's cinnamon and ginger notes always offered me a taste of familiarity, the feeling of home."

- 4 ounces soju
- 2 ounces cinnamon whiskey
- 2 ounces Domaine de Canton ginger liqueur
- 4 ounces Cinnamon Tea (recipe follows)
- 4 ounces Ginger Tea (recipe follows)
- 1 ounce freshly squeezed lemon juice
- 30 grams light brown sugar
- 5 ounces whole milk
- Garnish: 4 dried jujube wheels and pine nuts

Begin by clarifying the cocktail: In a large mixing container, combine all the ingredients, except the milk and garnishes, and stir to incorporate. Pour the milk into a separate large container. Slowly stream the spirit and tea mixture into the milk, stirring gently to combine. Allow the mixture to rest undisturbed for 1 hour at room temperature. During this time, the milk solids (curds) will separate from the liquid, trapping impurities and creating clarity.

To filter the cocktail, set a paper coffee filter over a large vessel. Carefully ladle or pour the mixture through the filter. The first few drops may appear cloudy—recirculate these through the filter until the liquid runs clear. Continue filtering slowly until the entire batch has passed through and the punch is fully clarified.

Serve each drink over a large block of ice in a rocks glass. Garnish with a thin wheel of dried jujube and a few pine nuts, for aroma and visual appeal.

continues →

8

ZERO PROOF

무알코올

KOREAN PALMER

SERVES 1

This is my take on an Arnold Palmer, traditionally a mix of iced black tea and lemonade. In this version, I swap in Yuja Honey Lemonade and green tea. The result is light and refreshing, with grassy undertones and a beautiful ombré effect.

4 ounces Yuja Honey Lemonade (recipe follows)
2 ounces Nokcha Cold Brew (page 94)
Garnish: Banana leaf (optional)

Pour the yuja honey lemonade into a pint glass over ice. Gently top with the cold brew to create a layered effect. Garnish with a banana leaf, if desired.

YUJA HONEY LEMONADE

MAKES 2 QUARTS

1 quart water
10 ounces Simple Syrup (page 32)
10 ounces freshly squeezed lemon juice
5 ounces yuja juice
5 ounces yuja citron honey

Whisk together all the ingredients in a large pitcher. Store in the refrigerator for up to a week.

NOTE: This lemonade can also be enjoyed spiked with your favorite vodka or gin.

SIKHYE SLUSHY

SERVES 3 OR 4

Sure, you *can* buy sikhye (rice punch) in cans or large bottles at the store, but you won't be able to achieve a level of maltiness strong enough to stand out in slushy form unless you make it at home. Traditional sikhye takes time, but my simplified version skips the rice maker and uses convenient, store-bought microwaveable rice.

Equipment: high-speed blender

210 grams malted barley flour (found online)

1 gallon lukewarm water

One 7.5-ounce package Korean cooked rice (found online)

1½ cups sugar, or to taste

Garnish: pine nuts

Combine the malted barley flour with the water in a large bowl and stir well. Cover and let ferment at room temperature for 2 hours. After 2 hours, carefully pour the liquid into an oven-safe pot with a lid, making sure not to disturb the sediment at the bottom of the bowl. Microwave the rice according to package instructions (usually about 1 minute), then add it to the pot. Gently stir to separate the grains without breaking them.

Cover the pot and place it in a 165°F oven. Let it ferment there for at least 6 hours—low and slow is key!

Remove the pot from the oven and transfer it to the stovetop. When you uncover it, the rice should have floated to the top. Use a strainer to scoop out as much of the rice as possible and set it aside.

Add the sugar to the liquid and simmer gently on the stove until the sugar dissolves. Remove from the heat, transfer to a heat-safe container, and stir the rice back in. Freeze until it's partially frozen and slushy-like. Check after an hour, then every 30 minutes, until you reach the perfect texture, 2 to 3 hours.

Transfer the mostly frozen slushy mixture to a high-speed blender and blend until smooth. Serve in glasses with pine nuts on top.

GRAPEFRUIT SHANDY

SERVES 1

Just because you abstain from alcohol doesn't mean you can't enjoy the pleasures of a shandy on a sunny deck. This nonalcoholic version, made with zero-proof beer, is a crisp and refreshing citrus delight, made special with the addition of a popular canned orange drink.

- 3 ounces pink grapefruit juice (store-bought or homemade)
- 1 ounce Sac Sac orange
- ¾ ounce Sujeonggwa Syrup (page 196)
- Top: 2 ounces Zero Gravity Rescue Club NA IPA, or nonalcoholic beer of your choice
- Garnish: 1 grapefruit wedge sprinkled with sea salt

Build the cocktail, except for the top and garnish, in a beer snifter and fill with ice. Swirl the contents with a mixing spoon. Top with the nonalcoholic beer and garnish with a grapefruit wedge.

BLACK SESAME SWIZZLE

HAN SUK CHO, MULTI AWARD-WINNING BARTENDER, FORMER BAR DIRECTOR, DIALOGUE, LOS ANGELES

SERVES 1

The inspiration behind Han Suk Cho's Black Sesame Swizzle came from the classic peanut butter and jelly sandwich. "I've always thought of sesame as the Korean equivalent of peanut butter," she says. The jelly comes in the form of maesil-cheong, a traditional Korean preserve made by sugaring unripe plums for at least six months.

4 ounces Black Sesame Milk (recipe follows)

1 ounce maesil-cheong

Combine the sesame milk and maesil-cheong in a highball glass and swizzle for 7 seconds with pebble ice. Top the glass with more pebble ice and a long straw.

BLACK SESAME MILK

MAKES 1 CUP

Equipment: high-speed blender

1 cup black sesame paste

1 cup water

Pinch of salt

Blend coarsely and strain through a cheesecloth-lined chinois. Add a pinch or two of salt to taste.

MY TALENTED FRIENDS

JAE BAE is a New York–based mixologist and influencer who draws millions of views on Instagram with his sensational cocktails based on savory dishes like tom yum soup and naengmyun.

HAN SUK CHO, a Los Angeles transplant, honed her skills as a chef before she was recognized by *San Franscisco Chronicle* for her creations as a nonalcoholic beverage director. She was named *Punch Magazine*'s Best New Bartender in 2023.

DONGJUN CHOI is owner and operator of Bar Cham in Seoul, ranked no. 6 in Asia's Best Bars of 2025. At his bar, Dongjun explores the diversity of soju, makgeolli, and fermentation in inventive ways through his cutting-edge cocktails.

SUNGRAE CHOI is head bartender at Seoul Salon and an alum of Momofuku Ko. Sungrae's program at Seoul Salon reimagines the traditional sool jib against the backdrop of New York City.

DYLAN "KENZO" HAN, currently based in Los Angeles, is the bar director of Firstborn, a buzzy, cool addition to its Chinatown locale. Kenzo was named one of *Punch Magazine*'s Best New Bartenders in 2025.

BENJAMIN HOPKINS is bar director of Brooklyn restaurants Agi's Counter and Pitt's, and my frequent collaborator in pop-ups. Ben is also a drinks writer and alum of Momofuku.

UNO JANG was born in South Korea and moved to Singapore, where he joined Jigger & Pony in 2017. As creative director, Uno played a key role in putting Singapore on the global cocktail map through the bar's many international accolades.

JOSEPH LEE is bar owner and creator of Antidote Bar in Seoul. Through prescription-inspired cocktail creations, Joseph manages to both thrill and cure whatever ails you.

SOPHIA KANG has brought her Seoul roots to Singapore's bar scene. As head bartender, Sophia pours her globally inspired cocktails at One-Ninety Bar with expertise and precision.

CHELSEA KIM is a Seoul-based bartender and three-time World Class Korea Top 10 finalist. Chelsea regularly shares updates on Asia's 50 Best Bars as a writer for domestic and international bar columns.

CHARLIE KIM is bar manager at Mo Bar, tucked away inside Mandarin Oriental in Singapore. Charlie is recognized for his commitment to zero-waste cocktail creation through his beverage program.

ROY KIM is owner, bartender, and team leader of Bar Pomme in Seoul, where he brings with him 17 years of mixology expertise and is dedicated to delivering exceptional cocktails through the bar's motto to "Sip, Savor, Awaken Senses."

JINOO KO previously oversaw the bar program at Oiji Mi in New York and has since moved up to his current role of general manager. Oiji Mi is a contemporary restaurant offering upscale Korean cuisine with a modern twist.

GREGORY KONG is a true born-and-bred New Yorker who has been making moves in the industry at mixology-forward establishments, such as Patent Pending. He is currently the bar director of Nomad Tea Parlor in New York.

SARAH KU cut her teeth slinging at Porchlight before joining GoldenHOF and NY Kimchi as beverage director, where she has crafted innovative Korean-inspired cocktails to complement the restaurants' refined pocha cuisine.

PAT PARK is CEO and cocktail mastermind of Pine & Co. in Seoul. Pat's bar succeeds in creating a unique and nostalgic place meant to transport guests back to the 1980s and '90s in Seoul.

KATRINA VANESSA SOBREDILLA led the bar program at 8282 in New York before branching out with creative pop-ups across the city. She is now the driving force behind the recently opened Ligaw.

SHARON YEUNG, currently based in Seattle, is the cocreator of the self-proclaimed "super Asian cocktail" pop-up @daijoubu.popup, bringing inventive events to cities across the country.

JENNIFER YIM, a Las Vegas–based cocktail consultant, has been inspired to continuously craft and execute the latest trends after being in the industry for the past 17 years. She is the cocreator of @spirit.n.seoul, a Korean-inspired cocktail pop-up.

INDEX

Printed in China
First Edition

For information about permission to reproduce selections from this book, write to Permissions, Countryman Press, 500 Fifth Avenue, New York, NY 10110

For information about special discounts for bulk purchases, please contact W. W. Norton Special Sales at specialsales@wwnorton.com or 800-233-4830

Manufacturing by TOPPAN Leefung
Book design by Allison Chi
Production manager: Devon Zahn

Countryman Press
www.countrymanpress.com

An imprint of W. W. Norton & Company, Inc.
500 Fifth Avenue, New York, NY 10110
www.wwnorton.com

Authorized EU representative: EAS, Mustamäe tee 50, 10621 Tallinn, Estonia

978-1-324-11181-8

1 2 3 4 5 6 7 8 9 0